An Introduction to the
Values of the Talmud

The
Wisdom
of Judaism

Rabbi Dov Peretz Elkins

For People of All Faiths, All Backgrounds

JEWISH LIGHTS Publishing

Woodstock, Vermont

The Wisdom of Judaism:
An Introduction to the Values of the Talmud

2007 First Printing
© 2007 by Dov Peretz Elkins

Library of Congress Cataloging-in-Publication Data
Elkins, Dov Peretz.
The wisdom of Judaism : an introduction to the values of the Talmud /
Dov Peretz Elkins.
p. cm.
ISBN-13: 978-1-58023-327-9 (pbk.)
ISBN-10: 1-58023-327-9
1. Talmud—Criticism, interpretation, etc. 2. Jewish way of life. 3. Jewish ethics. I. Title.
BM504.E63 2007
296.1'206—dc22

2006103352

10 9 8 7 6 5 4 3 2 1

Cover design: Tim Holtz
Cover art: S-166, "Maze-VIII of S.O.M. Suite," 1983 original color serigraph by Shraga Weil. Published by the Safrai Fine Art Gallery, Jerusalem, Israel. Copyright Safrai Gallery.

Manufactured in Canada

Published by Jewish Lights Publishing
A Division of LongHill Partners, Inc.
Sunset Farm Offices, Route 4, P.O. Box 237
Woodstock, VT 05091
Tel: (802) 457-4000   Fax: (802) 457-4004
www.jewishlights.com

To Our Children,

Hillel and Rachel
Jon and Rachel
Shira and Dany
Jamie and Abby
Yoni
Pesach

---

*"Children are a heritage from the Lord,
The fruit of the womb a reward."*

Psalm 127:3

CONTENTS

Part V

Part VI

"The final goal of wisdom is to turn to
God and to do good works."
                              Menahot 110a

———————

"The object of study is to teach true
values and sound judgment."
                    Rabbi Nachman of Breslov

ACKNOWLEDGMENTS

This is the third book I have edited or authored that Jewish
Lights has published. In each case I have had the stellar coopera-
tion, support, and wise guidance of many people, especially Stuart
M. Matlins, the visionary publisher of American Judaism today;
Emily Wichland, the talented and most helpful vice president for
editorial and production; and Lauren Seidman, senior project edi-
tor, whose daily e-mails I will miss when the book is finally fin-
ished. They are an unbeatable team, and it is a great pleasure to
work with each and all of them.

I also want to offer thanks to the following people who made
useful suggestions to improve the brief introductory essay on the
Talmud: Professor Raymond Scheindlin, Rabbi Charles Kraus,
Rabbi Shamai Kanter, Rabbi Steven Saltzman, and especially my
son Jonathan Elkins.

The Talmud—A Conversation Between Generations

Jewish literature is a conversation between generations. That's how a non-Jewish *New York Times* reporter described it when he interviewed my late professor, Rabbi Saul Lieberman, of blessed memory, and gazed at the massive collection of books on his shelves.

"What is that book?" asked the reporter.

"It's a commentary on the Bible."

"What's *that* book?" asked the reporter, pointing to another large tome on a different shelf.

"That's a commentary on the other commentary."

The conversation continued with six or seven questions and answers until the reporter realized that almost every book ever written in Judaism, from the Torah to the present day, is a commentary on another book.

"Aha!" exclaimed the reporter. "I see. In other words, Judaism is a conversation between the generations."

Because the heritage of the Jewish people includes a dynamic, ever growing, ever adapting body of literature, it almost seems as if each generation is holding an ongoing conversation with its predecessors. Each scholar, looking for answers to the unending questions that life presents all humans, searches for ideas in the stream of writings that came before. Then that scholar adds another volume. So Judaism indeed becomes a conversation between generations.

The Core Literature of the Jewish People

It started with the basic work, the covenant book, which, according to Jewish tradition, was given to Moses at Mount Sinai. The Torah, as it is known, contains five books—Genesis, Exodus, Leviticus, Numbers, and Deuteronomy. The Torah (or Pentateuch, which is Greek for "five books") is the divine source of all the other books that have since followed.

The Torah, the sacred anthology of cosmology, history, folklore, law, poetry, and genealogy, is the bedrock of all Jewish values, rituals, holidays and ideals. It covers the history of the nation of Israel from the first Jews, Abraham and Sarah, of eighteenth century BCE, all the way down to the second century BCE—about sixteen hundred years. When the last prophets uttered their divinely ordained thoughts, the Tanakh (the acronym for the three parts of the Hebrew Bible: Torah, N'vi'im [Prophets], and Ketuvim [Writings]) was canonized, or sealed, once and for all. Nothing more could be added or subtracted.

Like every book of law, customs, norms, and ideals, the Tanakh had to be interpreted, explained, and updated in every generation. When the holy Temple in Jerusalem was destroyed—first by the Babylonians in 586 BCE, and again by the Romans in 70 CE—the political and spiritual reins of the Jewish people shifted from priests and prophets to rabbis (teachers). The book of laws and teachings (the Torah) was given. The task now was to teach and interpret it, and to bring it up to date. Enter the Talmud.

Enter the Talmud

The Talmud, and its contemporary companion, the Midrash, were originally oral discussions that brought to bear the legal and homiletical interpretations of the postbiblical Rabbis, whose goal was to help their people make the Torah a more usable and understandable document. The first step in the creation of what is known as "rabbinic literature" was the Mishnah, compiled and edited by Rabbi Yehudah HaNasi, the head of the Sanhedrin (the legislative and judicial body in postbiblical times), in the year 200 CE.

By putting the Mishnah in writing, Rabbi Yehudah did something radical. Knowing that the passing of time would make it difficult for the people to remember all the continuing discussions of each generation, he set down on parchment, or perhaps papyrus, what was intended to be oral information passed from one generation to the next. He divided the laws of rabbinic Judaism into six orders and sixty-three tractates (approximately twelve or thirteen tractates per order).

Since the Torah and the comments on it were a scattered, disorganized collection of history, law, and lore, one of the great achievements of Rabbi Yehudah was to organize the material into themes. Thus, the Mishnah is divided into books about the various holidays, agricultural laws of ancient Palestine, civil and criminal law, issues between the sexes (such as marriage and divorce), sacrifices, and laws of purity.

Naturally, the process of expansion, explanation, and interpretation did not cease with the creation of the Mishnah. In the third century CE, a new group of rabbis began to discuss the passages in the Mishnah in a freewheeling, stream-of-consciousness dialogue that ultimately became the Gemara, which was edited in approximately the year 500 CE.

In common parlance, the Mishnah and the Gemara together are known as the Talmud. (There are two Talmuds: the Jerusalem Talmud, edited in approximately the year 400 CE, and the more comprehensive Babylonian Talmud, edited in approximately 500 CE, which is the one most people are referring to when they simply say "the Talmud" without qualification.) A page in a printed copy of the Talmud today contains a passage of the Mishnah followed by long, often disorganized debates and deliberations on the implications and conclusions derived from the Mishnaic passage. On the top, bottom, and sides of each page are many other commentaries written by later sages. Thus, "a conversation between the generations."

Deep within the sea of the Talmud are explanations of specific verses in the Torah. This genre of literature is known as *midrash*. There are two kinds of midrash—midrash halakhah (comments on legal matters) and midrash aggadah (homiletical or folkloristic matters). Some midrash is included within the folios of the Talmud and some midrashic comments are found in separate collections (such as Midrash Rabbah and Tanhuma).

Halakhah and Aggadah

In general, all of rabbinic literature can be divided into two categories: halakhah—legal discussions; and aggadah—folklore, myths, legends, stories, moral aphorisms, and other nonbinding advice and nonsystematic theology. The wisdom that is in these pages comes from the second category. We can certainly find many value statements embedded within the halakhic (legal) material of rabbinic literature, but that is a different collection and a separate approach.

What you will find in these pages is a small sampling of the countless teachings on life that are scattered throughout the Talmud and the Midrash. It is a taste to whet the appetite of interested readers so that they may begin to feast on the delightful banquet that is the Talmud—both the halakhic and aggadic sections.

Living the Good Life

This book focuses on some theological issues, such as God, miracles, ritual, and the meaning of religion. My main objective, however, is to show you that the ancient Rabbis were concerned most of all with living the good life. Each nation and culture throughout history has focused on its own callings: The ancient Greeks were pioneers in the fields of philosophy and drama; the Romans were experts in the areas of law and architecture; in later history, different European countries were interested in art and cuisine. The relentless passion of the Jewish people has been about how to grow the soul.

Professor Arthur Green once summarized this idea in the follow incident from his life:

> A number of years ago my family and I were living in Berkeley, California. Around the corner from us was, of course, a spiritual or New Age bookstore. The front of the store was decorated with a huge sign, in inverted pyramid form. The top line read, in large block letters: SCIENTOLOGY DOESN'T WORK. Beneath that, in slightly smaller letters, it said: INTEGRAL YOGA DOESN'T WORK. Then, again slightly smaller: CHRISTIANITY DOESN'T WORK. After going through six or seven more would-be spiritual paths the sign concluded, again in large letters: YOU WORK. Seeing this sign reminded me of a definition of Hasidism that Abraham Joshua Heschel had passed on in the name of the Kotsker rebbe. When asked what Hasidism was all about, Rabbi Mendel of Kotsk (Poland, 1787–1859) replied: "*Arbetn oif zikh*—to work on yourself" (from *Restoring the Aleph—Judaism for the Contemporary Seeker*).

Thus, the six sections of this book all deal in one way or another with matters of the heart and soul. How should we treat other people? What is the proper content of a "Jewish" conversation? How do we achieve fairness in dealing with all aspects of our lives? What makes a good marriage? What is the meaning of love?

Talmudic Themes

This introduction to Talmudic spiritual values is divided into the areas that I believe are considered primary in the worldview of the rabbinic mind. The first part deals with how to take responsibility for the welfare of others. Rabbi Israel Salanter, founder of the Musar Movement of Jewish ethics in the nineteenth century, once taught that good Jews should worry about their own soul and their neighbor's body. In other words, paying back to the community for all the rich blessings we receive is central to the human enterprise.

The second part, on human relationships, is an expansion of the laws that are found in the nineteenth chapter of Leviticus, the "Holiness Code." It spells out in great detail the obligations we have toward our neighbor.

Part three covers a variety of topics regarding the structure of the ethical life and how to achieve a high level of spiritual consciousness. Creating peace, being a humble person, mastering the art of flexibility, and the values of self-reliance and physical labor are some of the subjects explored.

The fourth part focuses on family values such as marriage, parenting, the home, and unconditional love.

Part five conveys the flavor of the rabbinical views on education, teaching and learning, and how best to assure the Jewish future by securely transmitting the Jewish heritage from one generation to the next.

Finally, we concentrate on a variety of dilemmas that every human being must confront in the course of life—the puzzles and enigmas of daily existence, such as the importance of emotions, the potential dangers of sin, and whether or not sinful behavior is irrevocable; and the relative importance of faith and belief compared to moral action.

Selecting the aphorisms was a difficult task, given the huge amount of ethical material found within the folios of Talmudic and Midrashic literature. They are reflections of my own learning and philosophy of life, as imparted to me by my teachers over the last fifty-plus years. The translations of the rabbinic passages are my own. I have tried my best to render ancient Hebrew and Aramaic phrases into felicitous modern English, without distorting their meaning or being too literal. Masculine language is sometimes retained in order to stay true to the original text, but this should not detract from the universal value of these sayings.

Rabbinic Style

There are certain characteristics of rabbinic literature that are useful to understand when reading the thoughts of scholars who lived approximately two thousand years ago. Above all, the ancient Rabbis were masterful pedagogues. Their maxims are brief, to the point, frequently contain a good deal of humor— sometimes hidden and sometimes blatant. They knew that to get a point across it is often necessary to exaggerate and make seemingly outrageous comparisons (for example, one aphorism states that earning a living is similar in difficulty to parting the Reed Sea). All the better to remember the teachings, and to call them up when similar situations arise in your own life.

Ageless Wisdom

Every commentary on the Bible, Talmud, and all classic Jewish literature deal with the same eternal questions: How can I apply these ancient texts to my own life in today's complex world? What significance and relevance does this idea, verse, chapter, or paragraph have for me? How can I use it in my day-to-day existence?

Much has changed from the days when the aphorisms in this collection were written. There were no televisions, computers, telephones, or airplanes then. The thousands of other technological, scientific, and medical advances were not even dreamed of.

But the human heart and soul have not changed. The *yetzer ha-ra,* the ubiquitous inclination to be selfish and destructive, are with us today as much as they were in ancient times. The Rabbis' understanding of how to behave, how to be kind, the importance of making personal sacrifices, how to treat parents and children, and the need to avoid shaming other people—and all the other myriad subjects that are dealt with in these pages—are acts that are timeless. In some cases it may take an open mind and a bit of modern thinking to apply an aphorism to your particular situation (where the Rabbis said "husband" or "wife" you may want to substitute "spouse" or "partner," for instance), but the values taught are as relevant to our times as they ever were—if not more so.

When a pagan approached the famous sage Hillel with the demand to "teach me all of Judaism while you stand on one foot," the master replied with these immortal words: "What is hateful to you, do not do to your neighbor. All the rest is commentary. Now, go and study!" It is time to seek out the commentary, to "go and study" the wisdom that has survived generations.

I

Kindness through Giving, Welcoming, and Sharing

"Deeds of kindness are equal to all the commandments."

Talmud Yerushalmi, Tractate Peah 1:1

THE ESSENCE OF RELIGION

The Torah begins and ends with acts of kindness.

Sotah 14a

The Torah bases itself on two stories: in Genesis God clothes the naked—God covers Adam and Eve with a leaf—and in Deuteronomy God buries Moses. (See a similar statement in Judaism's early morning *Shaharit* service, from Shabbat 127a: *Elu devarim she'adam okhel perotayhem* ... [These are the deeds that yield immediate harvest and continue to yield in future days...].)

Clothing the naked and burying the dead are among the acts of kindness frequently mentioned when the ancient Rabbis discuss the daily acts of goodness that every human being may be called upon to perform.

There are several things that stand out regarding this Talmudic passage.

First, it is not the gigantic, heroic, once-in-a-lifetime things we do that Judaism (and all religions, I believe) demands of us. It is the simple daily acts, the repetitive acts of goodness, thoughtfulness, and concern for the other, that make us "religious," that is, ethical and spiritual. Helping a neighbor, providing food for the hungry, giving clothes for the needy, and offering assistance with a life-cycle event—such as a birth, a wedding, or a burial—are the mark of the religious person in Judaism.

Second, what we call "the essence of religion" in Judaism is what we do for others. In a famous passage in the Jerusalem Talmud, God says that, if necessary, it is more important to treat our fellow humans well than it is to treat God well. God says, "I wish that when necessary, my children would forget me, and pay more attention to the Torah's ethics about treating one another" (Jerusalem Talmud, Hagigah 1:7).

As Martin Buber, the Austrian-Jewish philosopher, points out in *Hasidism and Modern Man*, this is one of the primary characteristics of Hasidic philosophy, which is to say that it is a Jewish doctrine that Hasidism emphasizes. In Buber's words, the core teaching of Hasidism is that "[You] cannot approach the divine by reaching beyond the human; [you] can approach [God] through becoming human. To become human is what [you have] been created for."

CHARITY IS BETTER
THAN SACRIFICE

**Giving tzedakah is greater than all
the sacrifices in the world.**

Sotah 49b

When the Temple in Jerusalem was destroyed by the Romans in 70 CE, the Jewish people were in chaos. Their capital shattered, the people exiled from their homeland, the House of God brought to ruins, what would happen to God's chosen people? This earthshaking event was the most significant occurrence in Jewish history, and the most terrible tragedy until the Shoah in the twentieth century. The question in the minds of the people was surely: How can we establish our connection with God without the holy Temple? Will Judaism survive without our having the ability to bring offerings of thanksgiving, sin, and guilt, and without the occasions for sharing with the *kohanim* (priests) our gratitude for the bounty at the seasons of harvest—Pesach, Shavuot, and Sukkot?

After centuries of struggling with these difficult and painful questions, the Rabbis decided that there were other means to approach God. There was: prayer, the study of Torah, acts of kindness, and the giving of tzedakah (charity).

By the third and fourth centuries, the Talmudic Rabbis had become accustomed to the notion that it would be a long time, if ever, before the sacrificial system was restored. They made peace with the idea that God would still be accessible to them through other means. In fact, in statements like the one about tzedakah that opens this chapter, it seems they even accepted the idea that there might be *better* ways to satisfy God and live a pious life than by making animal sacrifices and meal offerings. Helping those in need, be it financially or through other means, was surely pleasing to God.

Rabbinic hyperbole is well known. Any good teacher knows that a strong, even exaggerated, statement is likely to burrow its way into the mind of the student. We cannot know if the sage who declared that tzedakah is more important than sacrifice was making the best of a bad situation, or whether he had come to the mature realization, as Maimonides (twelfth-century rabbi, physician, and philosopher) did a millennium later, that the whole sacrificial system was merely a primitive stage in the evolution of Jewish religious ritual.

In any case, his statement is an important one, and it gives us, in the twenty-first century, confidence that our tradition contains the power of evolution and growth, and that we can aspire to even better ways to serve God as time passes. We need not be locked into ancient rituals whose usefulness has been replaced by more humane and humanistic practices.

HOSPITALITY TO THE NEEDY

Let the doors of your home be wide open,
and may the needy be often in your home.

Avot 1:5

A Jew who is not hospitable to the needy ignores one of the
most important mandates of the Jewish tradition. The first half of
this Talmudic quote reminds us that we should be hospitable to
all people. The second half reminds us that we need to be *especially* gracious and hospitable to the needy.

The practice of opening our doors to the needy goes as far back
as the founder of the Jewish people, Avraham Avinu—Abraham,
our father. In Genesis (Bereshit) 18:1–8 we read of Abraham's
graciousness to three strangers passing by his tent. As soon as he
sees them he runs to greet them, bows down, and pleads with
them to allow him to bring them some water to refresh their body
and soul, and some food to eat. The medieval commentators note
that even though Abraham could ask a servant to perform these
acts, he insists on doing them himself.

The Talmud informs us (Taanit 20b) that before each meal,
Rav Huna would publicly announce this proclamation, which
became part of the Passover seder: "Whoever is hungry, let them
enter and eat." Another rabbinic passage teaches that a host must

present a cheerful presence during meals (Derekh Eretz Zuta 9). And, following the example of Avraham Avinu, the host herself should serve at the table (Kiddushin 32b).

On a personal note, I can say that the few times I have traveled in Europe and attended synagogue on Shabbat and festivals, I have invariably been invited to someone's home for a meal. The same is true in Israel, where my family and I have been welcome guests in many homes—both of those with whom I have a relationship and those who recognized me as a stranger/visitor and approached me after shul asking if I had a place to have the Shabbat meal. While I hardly consider myself in the category of "needy," Jewish tradition also regards as needy someone who has no home (a hotel is hardly a home, and not the most *shabbasdik* place) to go to after religious services.

The age-old custom of warmth and hospitality in the Jewish tradition, I believe, rests on the assumption that all Israel is one family. A Jew who saw a brother or sister, an aunt or uncle, or a cousin who was traveling alone and had no place to eat a meal would invite that person home. When you consider every Jew part of your family, it goes without saying that hospitable treatment is to be expected in any such encounter—including encounters beyond the circle of the Jewish people. This is the way of the Jew.

Tzedakah Must Come
with Caring

Whoever gives a coin to the needy
is blessed with six blessings;
but one who comforts the needy with kindness
is blessed with twelve blessings.

Bava Batra 9b

Tzedakah is only complete when it comes with kindness.

Sukkah 49b

Teachers of Jewish ethics often point out the sharp distinction between the Jewish idea of helping the needy—tzedakah—and the Christian concept of charity—*caritas*, or pity. In other words, in Christianity a person gives because of a sense of compassion, while in Judaism a person gives because it is a duty, a commandment. The idea is that even if you are not in a charitable, or compassionate, mood, you must give anyway, and preferably 10 percent of your income (and not more than 20 percent, lest your obligation to the needy deprive you or your family of basic necessities).

The most poignant story I ever heard to illustrate this point is about a collector of tzedakah who looks into the window of the home of a certain man and overhears him telling his servant to go to the marketplace and buy the least expensive piece of fish he can find. The tzedakah collector skips knocking on that door because he doesn't expect to receive much from this needy family. At the end of the day he has not made his quota, so he goes back to that home anyway. To his surprise he receives a huge contribution. When he asks the master of the house why, earlier in the evening, he told his servant to buy a very inexpensive piece of fish but now gives such a generous charitable gift, the man answers, "When I buy for myself, I must be parsimonious, but when it comes to tzedakah I have no choice—it is a command from God."

However, this view does not reflect the whole story. True, a person must give whether the spirit moves the heart or not because it is a duty to give. However, Judaism also recognizes the psychological needs of the needy. Thus, our two statements above. Giving with kindness, caring, and understanding is also important. Giving is essential, but giving with heart is all the more so!

STRONGER THAN DEATH

Ten powerful things were created in the world:
A rock is strong, but iron smashes it;
iron is strong, but fire can melt it;
fire is strong, but water extinguishes it;
water is strong, but clouds absorb it;
clouds are strong, but the wind disperses them;
wind is strong, but a person withstands it;
a person is strong, but fear shatters him;
fear is strong, but wine dissolves it;
wine is strong, but sleep dispels it;
and stronger than all these is death!
Yet tzedakah can save from death!

Bava Batra 10a

The Tanakh claims that "love is strong as death" (Song of Songs 8:6). However, in this Talmudic riddle we find that tzedakah is stronger than death. It is not surprising that death is viewed by both the Tanakh and the Talmud as the most powerful force in the world. It puts a period to the sentence of life. Death inspires awe and fear now as it did in ancient times. But if the Rabbis wanted to ascribe strength to some force in the world, it would have to be stronger than death—the mightiest engine of power known to humans. Not surprising, again, is that the Rabbis chose a force that is spiritual—tzedakah. For tzedakah is not a physical, tangible object. It is not money. It is the act of helping a person in need. It is the right and the *righteous* thing to do. In other words, *righteousness* is more powerful than death. What a marvelous ethic!

The thing that humans fear most in the world can be ultimately defeated by a simple spiritual force that all of us are capable of performing: righteous living, sharing, giving, caring, and doing for our neighbors and others in need. The power of the human spirit, acting in a manner that transcends the forces of rock, iron, fire, wind, fear, wine, and death, is the most powerful force in the universe. "Not by might and not by power, but by Spirit alone," as songwriter Debbie Friedman translates Zechariah's phrase.

So much ink has been laid to parchment on the subject of tzedakah in the Jewish tradition, because it sums up all the values that our ancestors lived by and aspired to—a society in which all are cared for, and all have food to eat, clothing to wear, and lodging to shelter them. This glorious ideal can rise above our worst fear—that life ends and we are no more. But tzedakah keeps us alive, because the human spirit is indestructible and eternal. A worthy subject for a facile pen to poetically set down is the degrees of power that were created, but tzedakah trumps them all.

FINDING A GOOD HEART

What is the right path that one should cling to?
A good heart for heaven, and a good heart for humans.

Avot de-Rabbi Natan 14:5

It has been said that each nation, each culture, has its major mission. For the Romans it was buildings and roads; for the Greeks it was philosophy, sculpture, and drama; for the French it is food, wine, and *l'amour*. For the Jews it has always been "the good life." How does one find "the right path," one that will please God and please our neighbors?

Rabbi Yose the Galilean taught: "The impulse for good judges the righteous, as we read, 'My heart is pierced within me' (Psalm 109:22). The impulse for evil judges the wicked, as we read, 'Sin speaks to a wicked one within the heart'" (Psalm 36:2) (Berakhot 61b). Similarly, the Midrash teaches "The wicked are under the control of their hearts, but the righteous have their hearts under their control" (Bereshit Rabbah 34:1).

Both the Tanakh and the Talmud see the heart as the driver in moral behavior. We may call it "conscience," or "soul," but something God has planted within us wants us to be good human beings. Our task is to cooperate with the divine, to be God's partner in finding what is the best choice for the right circumstance.

13

Again from the Talmud: "The kidneys counsel, the heart discerns, the tongue speaks, the mouth articulates" (Berakhot 61a). In the rabbinic mind it is the heart that sees through the thick mass of confusion and discerns the truth, the best, the kindest path. "All parts of the body depend on the heart" (Jerusalem Talmud, Terumah 8:10).

Among all his students, Rabban Yohanan ben Zakkai preferred the words of Elazar ben Arakh, who said that a person must cultivate an unselfish heart (Avot 2:10).

How often do young people struggle with moral questions and turn to a wise elder for help in finding a solution—only to be told to follow their hearts? A person with a good heart will overcome whatever obstacles life puts in his or her path, and find a way to lead a life that sparkles with sweetness, compassion, integrity, and honor. This is the Jewish mission and the Jewish passion.

THREE IMPORTANT
JEWISH VALUES

This [Jewish] people is recognized by three qualities:
They are compassionate, they are modest,
and they perform acts of lovingkindness.

Y'vamot 79a

This passage is a powerful statement of the mission of the Jewish people. Does it mean that every Jew in the world possesses all three of these qualities in full measure at all times? Doubtful. I see these as a combination of a historical judgment and an ideal. The Rabbi who wrote this is saying that our tradition asks us to try to emulate these three qualities as much and as often as possible. I think he is also saying that if we look back at the history of the Jewish people, these are the qualities they have lived by, if not always in perfect measure.

First and foremost, notice that there is no ritual performance in this list of qualities that a Jew must live up to. They are all moral qualities, or ethical values.

Next, let's look at each of these and see if we can flesh them out a bit.

Compassion is a trait that covers a multitude of moral and honorable qualities. Someone who is compassionate is empathic, caring, and loving. Someone who is compassionate is slow to anger (understanding, rather than condemning or criticizing), patient, and focused on how to be of help. In the Jewish heritage, action is primary; thus, compassion must include a strong component of reaching out and doing concrete acts of caring and helping, not just feeling good thoughts in the heart.

Modesty is not a precise translation of the Hebrew *bayshan*, but it comes as close as possible. *Bayshan* is used in modern Hebrew to mean a person who is shy or bashful. In the context of this statement, that is clearly not the intent of the author. The connotation here is someone who is modest, which might mean a person who displays characteristics of decency, dignity, integrity, and high moral principles, including such things as appropriate dress, language, and demeanor. It would rule out the kind of things we see in the media today, in Hollywood and on television, in terms of dress and language. The Hebrew word *tz'niyut* comes to mind. *Bayshan* also connotes behavior that is reserved rather than boisterous or loud, a person who is modest, humble, and unpresumptuous. Too often we act out with attention-seeking behavior and lose sight of these qualities. This Talmudic statement might serve as a useful corrective for modern society's looseness and laxity in these matters.

Acts of lovingkindness include a wide range of behaviors that are characteristic of traditional Jews. The Talmudic passage quoted in the *Shaharit* (morning) service includes some of the primary acts that encompass the meaning of *gemilut hasadim*, or acts of lovingkindness. The Talmud informs us (Shabbat 127a) that we receive special rewards for doing such things as honoring our parents, showing hospitality to strangers, visiting the sick, helping a needy bride, attending the dead, and making peace between people. There is a special society in Jewish communities—known as a *Gemach*, an abbreviation of *gemilut hasadim*—whose mission it is to perform such acts.

Any time you wonder what it means to be a good Jew, this Talmudic statement gives an answer that is sound, traditional, and fulfilling.

LOVE PEACE AND PURSUE PEACE

Be among the disciples of Aaron—
love peace and pursue peace,
love humanity,
and bring them close to the Torah.

Avot 1:12

Scholars and commentators have had mixed views about Aaron. The harsh view is that he would do anything to please the people. When Moses ascended Mount Sinai for forty days, Aaron acceded to the people's wishes to make a Golden Calf, which in turn wreaked havoc among the people and brought down severe punishment from God. The kinder view is that Aaron was a peacemaker, helping to mollify the anger of the mob and bring tempers to a more even keel. Rabbinic midrash takes the kinder view. One legend has it that when Aaron knew of two people who were angry at each other, he would approach each and say, "Your opponent is interested in making peace." The two adversaries would quickly make peace, not knowing that this was a ploy concocted by Aaron to get the two to see beyond their (perhaps) irrational emotions.

Commentators point out that there are two verbs in the first sentence of this passage: to love peace and to pursue peace. The first is more passive, the latter more active. We can love peace in the abstract and do nothing to bring it about. Peace will not come unless we work for it, or pursue it. Loving something is not sufficient; it must be achieved.

The next two *stichs* (lines) share the same pattern. A disciple of Aaron should love people, but loving them is not enough. If you love others, you should do something positive for them. If you are a believer in the efficacy and potency of the Torah, you should make an effort to bring others closer to the Torah. Thus, a disciple of Aaron will help a friend see the beauty and meaning of a life of Torah. Of course, there is a fine line between advising a friend and missionizing. Jewish tradition has always advocated a gentle approach to conversion. We can help a person who is interested in becoming Jewish, but throughout most of Jewish history, it was not common to aggressively go after others to convert them from their religion to Judaism. Bringing someone close to Torah does not necessarily imply bringing a non-Jew to the Jewish faith. It also includes bringing Jews closer to their own heritage. *Keruv*, a widely acclaimed movement today, includes both helping non-Jews—especially intermarried non-Jews—be accepted within the Jewish community and helping unaffiliated or uninterested Jews become more active and involved in Jewish life. Those who participate in either kind of *keruv* can be considered disciples of Aaron.

Whether one judges Aaron harshly or gently, it is always a good thing to love and pursue peace, to love people, and to bring them closer to Torah values.

EMBARRASSING OTHERS

**Whoever shames another in public
is like one who sheds blood.**

Bava Metzia 58b

It is true that the ancient Rabbis, who were superb pedagogues, had a predilection for hyperbole. Just about the worst thing one person can say about another is that a crime committed by that person is equivalent to murder. There is a clear implication, in this passage, that embarrassment resembles murder because shaming someone in public causes that person's face to whiten, as the facial blood restricts within the arteries. This is, literally, "shedding blood."

But in addition to the metaphoric implication of "shedding blood" by altering the visage, the Rabbis surely believed that shaming another is one of the most serious sins a person can commit. A book can be written about all the statements made by the Talmud and the Midrash that relate to shaming another person. The Rabbis were extraordinarily diligent about preserving the self-respect and dignity of others. Their high ethical standards went far beyond the prohibition of physical harm. Psychological harm, they correctly understood, was as bad, and sometimes worse, than physical harm. Would you not prefer to have someone punch you in the stomach than humiliate or shame you before friends, colleagues, or community?

Shaming a person leaves an indelible scar. A physical wound may heal in time, but a wound on the soul is less likely to fade and heal. Perhaps it all goes back to the biblical notion of the worth of a human being. We humans are made in the image of God, and any diminution of someone created in the image of God is no different than demeaning God. Preserving the dignity of a fellow human, whatever the effort and cost, is always considered worth the endeavor. No child of God should be subjected to an act of shame or humiliation by a fellow human being. I've heard people say in exasperation, "I'd rather die than be embarrassed in public." This is precisely the point of the Rabbis—that public humiliation is as bad as murder. Perhaps worse. This seemingly harsh warning is not too stern when we consider the high level of dignity attributed to all of God's creatures.

SENSITIVITY TO OTHERS

If you did a little harm to your neighbor,
let it be in your eyes as if it were much.
And if you did a great good to your neighbor,
let it be in your eyes as if it were only a little.
And if your neighbor did a small good thing for you,
let it be in your eyes as if it were a great thing.
And if your neighbor did a very bad thing to you,
let it be in your eyes as if it were of little import.

Avot d'Rabbi Natan 41:11

This statement is about two ways in which humans relate to others. The first involves perception, and the second involves ego.

The way we perceive our own actions in relation to others has a powerful influence on our expectations. If we believe we have done some wonderful action for a friend, we will expect to receive something similarly wonderful in return. Conversely, if we believe that our friend did something small or unimportant for us, the likelihood is that when it comes our turn to reciprocate, we might do something inconsequential for that person.

Thus, the wise Rabbi/psychologist is attempting to alter our perception of our own deeds and that of our neighbors' actions.

Along with the perception of the act follows the consequence. Thus, if we see something we did to another as relatively minor, we will brush it off without an apology, without feeling uncomfortable, and without a need to make amends. Perception accounts for so much, and the author of this statement intuitively realized that what follows large or small acts depends a great deal on the perception of the doer as well as that of the receiver.

For example, if we make an offhand comment to someone that we consider to be nothing more than an aside, we will be rather surprised if the person replies that he or she was hurt or insulted. This can easily escalate into hurt feelings, cool relations, further hurtful comments, and the likelihood of distancing from one another—all because we consider what we did or said to be minor, small, and unimportant. So our Rabbi-adviser warns us to consider everything we say or do to another person to be of great importance. Because in the final analysis, it is the listener, the receiver, whose subjective feelings count. Whether we intended it to hurt, harm, or cause bad feelings is not the point. It is the effect on the other person that really counts.

There is another human personality trait that also gets in the way of positive human relations, and that is our ego. In modern times, living in a free and open society in which every child knows that the American Constitution and Declaration of Independence guarantee "life, liberty and the pursuit of happiness," our egos have been inflated beyond the boundaries of an ethically sensitive human being. The net effect of this is that we too often feel that everything we do is very important, helpful, and deserving of praise, appreciation, and reciprocation. At the same time, whatever our friends and neighbors do to us is magnified into something that is awful, hurtful, and undeserved—in fact, deserving of a harsh response.

A person who possesses sensitivity, humility, and compassion is much more able to relate maturely and effectively to other human beings. A powerful suggestion and a good start in relating in these ways is to reduce the perception we have of our own magnanimity while enhancing our perception of the small acts of goodness and kindness that others do to and for us.

KINDNESS TO ANIMALS

**One must not put any food in one's mouth,
until the animals have been fed.**

Gittin 62a

The Torah and rabbinical literature are filled with statements that show kindness to animals. In Deuteronomy, for example, we find such laws as the prohibition against muzzling an ox while plowing. Doing so would speed up the ox and provide more food for the farmer, but it would be cruel to the animal. In another verse we find a prohibition against putting a yoke on one slow animal with one faster animal. This would make it difficult and painful for the slow animal to do its work.

Other laws and comments about treating animals kindly can be found throughout the breadth of Jewish literature.

I am particularly drawn to this statement about feeding our pets and other animals before filling our own mouths. First, it is simple, direct, and concrete. Second, as we will see, it is a repetitive act, and therefore has powerful educational value. Third, it is counter-intuitive, and while few people would object to its fairness, many are surprised that such a law exists in Jewish literature.

Let me explain what I mean by each of these. First, many of the ethical maxims in Jewish and general literature are theoretical, express kind, compassionate, and righteous thoughts, but have no immediate, visible, or practical results. By contrast, this law must be carried out on a regular basis and is a clear mandate of action.

Second, because animals usually had to be fed three or more times a day, the repetition serves as a potent reminder of the ethical implications contained in the process. It is therefore a very effective tool to train people to be thoughtful, sensitive, and compassionate to all living creatures, and not only to pets and other animals. The more you repeat an ethical action, the more deeply ingrained it is in your soul. Something that occurs several times each day (such as eating) is the best educational tool available to reinforce high-minded principles.

For that reason I believe the practice of *kashrut* is an important way to teach ethical values and Jewish awareness. I frequently remind couples in premarital interviews that since a young child in a kosher home has to remember to go to the right drawer or shelf to get flatware and dishes, it is a frequent and constant reminder of the child's Jewish identity. If the ideals of *kashrut* are taught in the home, school, or synagogue, its practice will be a constant reminder that eating is a sacred and ethical act. Anyone eating kosher meat should be reminded that the animal that was killed for this meat to be on the table was killed in a painless and humane fashion, so that a repugnance for consuming (and shedding) blood is built into the Jewish psyche.

By the same token, making sure our animals are fed before we put a morsel in our mouths is a sensitizing act that teaches the sanctity of, and respect for, all living creatures. It also reinforces the idea that the act of eating in Judaism is considered a sacred ritual, and not just a bodily need. Since we usually eat at least three times a day, we are constantly reminded of the ethical principle to treat animals kindly.

Lastly, I very much like the idea that this is a Jewish law that few would have thought of, or would find in many other cultures and religions, and that it is not something that easily comes to the minds of pet owners. In this instance, I believe Judaism teaches something that is unique to its culture. If that is the case, it is also a value that the average ordinarily ethical, thinking, rational, democratic, and compassionate human being might otherwise not think of if the command had not appeared in the corpus of Jewish law.

For me, this reemphasizes the notion that the Jewish people have sought to improve ethical practice over the centuries. The Jewish obsession has always been with the highest level of moral behavior, and this law adds weight to that assertion.

II

Human Relationships: Treating Others Fairly, Openly, and Lovingly

"Rabbi Simlai declared, 'The Torah begins and ends with acts of lovingkindness.'"

Sotah 14a

MODERATION

**Always let your left hand push away,
and your right hand pull toward you.**

Sotah 47a

Judaism has always been known for its emphasis on moderation. In the Middle Ages, the great philosopher Maimonides, who was strongly influenced by Aristotelian ethics, identified ideal behavior with the Golden Mean. In his view, to follow balanced behavior in life is to fulfill the mitzvah of walking in God's ways (Mishneh Torah, Hilkhot De'ot 1:5). A word like "mainstream" reflects the theology and psychology of Jewish law, lore, and life. In most areas of life this is sage, strong, and useful advice.

It may be true that on some occasions being in the middle is considered "sitting on the fence." There is the (Yiddish) expression that only a horse walks in the middle of the road. But that is not the intent of this Talmudic saying. There may be times when lack of passion results in a point of view that is too weak to be either liberal or conservative. But in most situations, what is important is to avoid the extremes. This is the danger we face today—apathy on the one hand, and fanaticism on the other. Each carries its own particular risks.

A seasoned, thoughtful, and carefully considered approach is usually what is called for. As a counselor and therapist, I have been trained to listen prudently to both sides in a dispute—whether in marriage counseling or in any difference of opinion. As a rabbi, I am sometimes challenged by lay leaders with a report of a disgruntled congregant, and my answer is inevitably, "Have you heard the other side of the story?" Carefully weighing each side is crucial to the resolution of any conflict or incidence of dissatisfaction.

This statement in the Talmudic tractate of Sotah is designed to treat a sinner with tough love. We should be firm with such a person, yet not too overpowering. We should also reach out with love to a sinner in the hope that the person will reform.

The Talmudic statement is reminiscent of the way a rabbi is enjoined to respond to someone who wishes to convert to Judaism. The rabbi is told to warn the prospective convert of the dangers and discomforts of being a member of an unpopular minority group, and to remind the individual of the anti-Semitism, the discrimination, and the loneliness that often accompany the life of a Jew. Thus, we should "push away" with one hand. Yet, with the other hand, we are advised to be warm, accepting, encouraging, and helpful so that we do not appear to be aloof, arrogant, exclusivist, and rejecting. This is the "pull."

The advice regarding conversion to Judaism is applicable to any difficult life-changing decision. A good advisor should always help an ambivalent person see both sides of a new possibility or idea. The assumption is that with some pushing and pulling in both directions, after a while the questioning person will find a comfortable middle ground.

TURNING AN ENEMY
INTO A FRIEND

Who is the greatest of all heroes?
One who turns an enemy into a friend.

Avot d'Rabbi Natan 23:1

Being among the smallest and weakest nations of the world for most of its history, the Jewish people has relied on its inner spirit, its intelligence, and its moral power. Recall the words of the biblical prophet Zechariah: "'Not by might, nor by power, but by My spirit,' says Adonai *tz'va-ot*" (4:6). This has been a dominant theme in Jewish history. The statement under discussion presents one example of how using moral power helps to lift us above the average level of morality.

First we have to look at the Hebrew word for "hero," *gibor*, which reflects power. In most cases it is raw, physical strength that is referred to. The effectiveness of this Talmudic principle, then, is the contrast it draws between one kind of strength and another. In fact, it redefines the concept of strength. The highest kind of strength, the Rabbi argues, is not brute power, but moral muscle. Someone who can achieve an enormous act of strength without lifting a finger, but rather by exercising clear judgment, engaging in compassionate and empathic listening, and using finely tuned skills in negotiation and conflict resolution—such a person is the most powerful person in the world.

This new definition of power is a revolution in world thinking, for which the most common method of resolving conflict has been war, or, in modern times, overcoming an opponent with disproportionately powerful and destructive weapons. The Rabbi is teaching us that there is a higher level of strength—inner strength. Instead of vanquishing our enemy, we should try to bring the enemy to our side. This does not mean our ideological opponents must agree with everything we believe and think. It merely points out that people can learn to disagree without being disagreeable. Whether our disagreement revolves around ideology, land, or economic control, we need not incapacitate or eliminate the other. We can, and indeed we must, indulge in creative dialogue, agreeable argumentation, philosophical sparring, and other nonphysical means in order to bring about a peaceable resolution to the conflict.

There is an underlying assumption in this Talmudic assertion that beneath all anger is a corps of people who are interested in coming closer to one another, as opposed to being enemies or adversaries. There are many times when our anger is aroused, or when our turf feels invaded or assaulted, and our first reaction is to demand our rights. This often leads to bickering, and perhaps next, to physical confrontation. But maturity demands that we rise above our initial reactions and find a way to settle any differences or disagreements. This is not an easy thing to do. We are creatures of emotion, which is good. We have an instinct for self-protection, which is positive. But when emotions and a worthy desire for self-protection are exaggerated, there can be negative consequences. This is where the real hero steps in and enables others to overcome these initial reactions, and to find a level of ground that is higher than the one on which we first find ourselves. When we do find that higher ground, it is possible and desirable to turn an enemy, or a potential enemy, into a friend, who is likely to become a better friend than we could have expected.

COMMUNITY

Either community or death!

Taanit 23a

This popular saying is quoted at the end of a fascinating myth in the Talmud about Honi the Circle Drawer, a magical rainmaker. Honi falls asleep for seventy years. Brush grows around him so no one notices, and his "death" is reported so no one questions his absence. When he awakens, he discovers that no one recognizes him and that seventy years have passed. He goes to his home and asks if the son of Honi the Circle Drawer is still alive. The answer is no, but his grandson is. Frustrated, he goes to the *bet midrash* (house of study) and announces himself, but no one believes him. Not receiving the respect and camaraderie of his colleagues, Honi the Circle Drawer asks to die, and he does. The Rabbis then repeat the popular saying, "Either community or death!"

The phrase is often quoted without the context because it stands by itself. Its meaning is plain and clear and almost needs no commentary. We can hardly participate in Jewish study without companions with whom to share ideas, debate issues, and act as sounding boards. Among Judaism's many wise and well-tested practices is the custom of studying Talmud with a partner—called a *hevruta*. Anyone who has ever seen a *bet midrash* will have memories of a cacophony of pairs throughout the room reading, reciting, correcting, testing, reviewing, and repeating. It's fairly amazing how dozens—and sometimes hundreds—of people can sit in the same room and talk to one other person about a serious issue in the Talmud with so much noise all around them.

In short, study of Jewish texts is a community enterprise, not a solo venture. But there is a broader meaning to this statement, for it is not only Jewish study that requires community. So, too, do prayer and a plethora of other Jewish religious, cultural, and social acts. A Jew cannot truly live out the mandates of Jewish life without sharing important spiritual experiences with like-minded individuals. Being Jewish requires community. Every Jew knows what a minyan is, and likewise, every Jew knows that prayers such as Mourner's Kaddish cannot halakhically be recited without one. We could make a very long list of Jewish activities, in addition to study and prayer, that simply are not the same without the participation of other Jews: observing Shabbat and festivals (in home and synagogue), doing acts of *tikkun olam* (social action, or, literally, "repairing the world"), educating our children, promoting the welfare of Israel, and so on.

"Either community or death!" can be taken literally, but its deepest meaning is that there is no life without sharing our most important, meaningful moments with other like-minded people. Without the intense give-and-take of collegial interaction on a significant level, life becomes either impossible or dull and tedious. Conversely, for people who live by common ideals and a dream of a shared destiny, study, prayer, and the pursuit of meaning are some of the most exciting things a human being can experience.

What Is "Jewish" Conversation?

One should always part from another
with a *"d'var halakhah,"*
since by doing so he will remember him.

Berakhot 31a

We could reflect on many possible lessons from this interesting observation. First, let's define our terms. A *d'var halakhah* is a discussion about some aspect of Jewish law. The assumption is that a person saying good-bye would give a personal interpretation of some intricate legal issue in the Talmud or post-Talmudic literature. Since halakhah (Jewish law) covers all aspects of civil and criminal law, and since the study of the law has been a major preoccupation of students, rabbis, and scholars from the earliest days of the existence of the Jewish people, we can easily imagine how many possible unsettled halakhic issues remain to be resolved.

Now let us try to "unpack" the meaning of this bit of advice. If discussing issues of Jewish law has been a predominant preoccupation of Jews for centuries and millennia, then it stands to reason that engaging in such a discussion would be a most appropriate way for two friends to occupy time. Next, we could ask this logical question: Why would Jewish law be grist for discussion at the moment of parting? The Talmudic statement itself supplies the answer—so that the friend parting will be engrossed in thought about what he has just heard, and he will keep his friend's words, and thus his friend's thoughts, ideas, and philosophy, in mind. There would also be a sense of appreciation within the listener for having just learned some new piece of Torah, thereby increasing the likelihood of his feeling closer to that person. According to this expression, by doing so, a person will not easily forget this friend and learning partner. We more easily forget people whom we care less about, and with whom we have little connection. By establishing a serious intellectual discussion, one more bond exists to make the friendship that much stronger.

A final thought about this statement, and perhaps the most important one: it seems to me that the real topic of discussion is, what should be the most prominent theme of discussion between friends? (In fact, the context of this statement in tractate Berakhot is that a person should focus on serious matters in personal discussion.) One of the criteria I use in selecting friends is asking myself what the usual fodder is for discussion between me and the other person. Do we just chatter about the weather, politics, and the latest movies? Or is there usually also some discussion about serious matters? I have been blessed to be in the company of people who hold important positions in academia, government, business, the media, and the arts. Living in Princeton, New Jersey, where one of the best universities in America is located, and where the nonuniversity residents are not far removed intellectually from the university crowd, has been a great blessing because it affords me the opportunity to engage in serious discussion with world-class intellectuals. My wife refers to this community as "Academia Heaven." But a person need not have advanced degrees to be interested in serious matters. And that, truly, is what I think this Talmudic dictum is all about. Namely, serious discussion.

Often I have watched people of substance turn a conversation from trivial noise into an elevated discussion of what Jewish tradition refers to as "things that stand at the heights of worldly matters" (Berakhot 6b). When you have a serious discussion that makes an impression, there is no better, or more powerful, way to establish bonds of friendship and to cement a relationship.

EQUALITY OF ALL
GOD'S CHILDREN

**Never consider a blessing of an ordinary person
unimportant to you.**

Megillah 15a

The Talmud lists a variety of sayings by distinguished rabbis, and this is one of them, by Rabbi Eliezer. Evidence of it is provided by citing two examples—blessings given to King David and to Daniel—from different places in the Tanakh. The Talmud says that these simple blessings, by undistinguished people (politically important people—kings, in fact—but not giants in spirit), turned out to have merit. David's and Daniel's blessings eventually were, in fact, realized.

There are surely many lessons that can be learned from Rabbi Eliezer's statement. What appeals to me about it is the notion that a kindness from an ordinary person should not be taken lightly. Too often our society is divided into social classes, set apart according to wealth, political influence, reputation, levels of education, fancy clothing, houses, cars, and other material criteria. The Talmud impresses upon us the equality of all of God's children. In the words of Pulitzer Prize–winning journalist George F. Will, "It is extraordinary how extraordinary the ordinary person is."

The opinions, feelings, good wishes, and praise of an ordinary person should be considered as important as that of the most prestigious individual in society. Like other people, I bask in the attention given me by distinguished people. My study is littered with photos of me standing next to prime ministers, presidents, and world-class artists and intellectuals. On occasion I ask myself if I think these make me any more important than I really am. The answer, of course, is no. The fact that I have my mug plastered on the wall next to Ed Koch, Marvin Hamlish, Jimmy Carter, Shimon Peres, and Alan Dershowitz gives me a quick shot of adrenaline when I'm feeling down, but it does nothing for my spiritual growth. If I were a bigger person, I might take more pride in hanging a photo of myself giving tzedakah to a poor Israeli kid in the street, or helping a disabled woman in Harlem get out of her wheelchair. But I guess I'm not much different from others in that respect. Many people love to be seen mixing with the powerful champions of society, the movers and shakers of the universe whose opinions make headlines.

This Talmudic statement offers a wonderful reminder to our inflated egos and our neurotic craving for glory and fame. I constantly revert to what I think is the most important sentence written any time, any place, which is Genesis 1:27—that each and every one of us is made in the image of God. None of us is more or less divine in origin than any other. Every life is equally sacred and infinitely and immeasurably holy. This is a message we need to hear, and hear again, on a daily basis.

PERSONAL GROWTH

Improve yourself,
and only afterward, try to improve others.

Bava Metzia 107b

As a trained marriage and family counselor, I have noticed that the prevalent attitude of people in relationships is: "If only he/she would change, everything would be fine." We are always pointing a finger at someone else. Sometimes, when trying to make the point that we need to start with ourselves, I ask people to stretch out their hand and point with their index finger. Then I ask them to notice where the third, fourth and fifth fingers are pointing. These three fingers are pointing back at themselves. Whenever we point the finger at someone else, I explain, we are at the same time pointing three fingers at ourselves. And in truth, the only person we can truly change is ourselves.

There is a wonderful Hasidic tale that illustrates this point. A famous Hasidic rebbe once proclaimed that when he was a young rabbi, his idealistic and romantic goal was to change the world. After a while, he realized that his aspiration was too grandiose, and so he lowered his expectations and said that he would be satisfied if he could just change his own community. After a while, realizing that even this goal was too ambitious, he settled for a wish to change his own congregation. Soon after, seeing that this was not so easily done, he said he would be satisfied if he could change his own family. When that task became too daunting for him, he finally confessed, "Now my goal is to change only myself, and do you know, I am not so sure anymore if even that is possible!"

The Talmudic statement we are examining is based on a common human tendency to view all wrongs in the world as the fault of everyone but yourself. To tell the truth, it is much easier to ascribe fault to others than to accept it as our own. The Jewish rite of passage that marks the entrance into adulthood, bar/bat mitzvah, differentiates the time when responsibility for a person's actions is transferred from one generation to the next.

Responsibility is the operative word. Bar/bat mitzvah is a major ceremony in Jewish life because it marks an emotional, spiritual, and halakhic milestone whose primary goal is to help a young person begin the lifelong process of what Carl Jung, founder of analytical psychology, called *individuation*. Similarly, Rabbi Mordecai Kaplan, founder of Reconstructionist Judaism, once said that we are not yet human, but rather we are candidates for humanity.

One of my teachers in the counseling process described the process of psychotherapy as "the unfinished business of growing up." It is my belief that very few people are truly grown up. Most of us remain, throughout our lives, in a state of stretching toward a higher level of maturity. We humans are prone to be self-serving, self-focused, and, at bottom, afraid of facing reality. The easiest way out of our dilemmas is to point a finger and blame others. But the wisest way, according to the Talmud, is to face up to the truth and begin the arduous lifelong process of changing ourselves. It is truly amazing what the effect of changing our own behavior can have on another person's actions. Changing ourselves, after all, is all we can really do. The rest, we hope and pray, will follow.

THE DANGERS OF PROJECTION

A fault that's in you,
be careful not to ascribe to another.

Bava Metzia 59b

Projection is one of the oldest psychological phenomena known to humankind. Its dangers have been recognized for millennia and have been dwelled upon in recent times as if they were discovered just yesterday. It has even been the object of humor. Woody Allen once observed, "My wife was very immature. Whenever I was in the bathtub she came and sank my little ships." Freud and Jung weighed in on the subject in their own ways. The father of psychoanalysis wrote, "We hate the criminal and deal severely with him because we view, in his deed, as in a distorting mirror, our own instincts." His student Carl Jung, who later broke with Freud and went off in his own direction, stated the benefits of projection in those who recognize it for what it is. He wrote: "Everything that irritates us about others can lead us to an understanding of ourselves." The flip side of this is that when we lack self-awareness, we are in the danger zone. As Solomon Schechter, the influential second president of The Jewish Theological Seminary of America put it, "It is ignorance of one's own errors that makes one ready to see errors of others."

All of these observations make the same point as our Talmudic warning—be careful not to assume that another's fault is of his making, and not of yours. What you see in your friend is perhaps nature's way of holding up a mirror to your own personality. A simple way to sum up this principle in human relations is that we do not see things as they are, but as *we* are. We project onto the screen of our vision what is in our own eye. A popular book on anger written several decades ago by humanitarian Laura Huxley was titled *You Are Not the Target,* implying that an angry person is projecting her annoyance toward another person instead of "owning" the anger she feels toward herself.

Lest we think that the phenomenon of projection is the subject of attention only in ancient and modern times, let's turn the clock back a few centuries and look at the thoughts of two wise observers of human nature. The famed Baal Shem Tov (1700–1760), legendary founder of Hasidism, is reputed to have said that when we see faults in sinners, we should realize that they only reflect the evil in ourselves. In other words, our personalities are primed to look for weaknesses in others when these faults are ones with which we are already well acquainted. Across the Atlantic Ocean, and a century after the Baal Shem Tov, Ralph Waldo Emerson offered teachings that were remarkably similar: "People seem not to see that their opinion of the world is also a confession of character. We can only see what we are, and, if we misbehave, we suspect others."

There is a German tale that is a good illustration of the problem with projection. A man whose axe was missing suspected his neighbor's son. The boy walked like a thief, looked like a thief, and spoke like a thief. But the man found his axe while he was digging in the valley, and the next time he saw his neighbor's son, the boy walked, looked, and spoke like any other child.

I also chuckle at the observation of twentieth-century writer Oren Arnold that "Human nature is something that makes you swear at a pedestrian when you are driving and at the driver when you are a pedestrian." Lack of self-awareness truly poisons our perceptions. The Rabbi of Lelov always told his students: You cannot be redeemed until you recognize the flaws in the soul and try to mend them.... Whoever permits no recognition of his flaws ... permits no redemption. We can be redeemed to the extent to which we recognize ourselves.

The ancient Rabbis possessed so much psychological sophistication that it's uncanny. But more than that, they had a thriftiness of language that eludes all the other writers and thinkers mentioned in this brief analysis. The Talmudic statement in its original Hebrew is but five words.

FEEDBACK

**If your neighbor calls you a donkey,
quickly get a saddle for your back.**

Bava Kama 92b

This Aramaic saying is a variant of a maxim that has circulated in various cultures for millennia. I was frankly surprised to read it in the Talmud, written some two thousand years ago. I had heard a different version of it in the 1970s, when I did training at workshops sponsored by various institutions fostering personal and spiritual growth. The one I heard went something like this:

If one person tells you that you are a donkey, you can laugh at them. If two people tell you that you are a donkey, give it some serious thought. If three people tell you that you are a donkey, go buy a saddle.

The main difference between the two versions is that the modern form recognizes that not all feedback is valid and you must distinguish between insults, off-the-cuff comments, and useful advice. What are the criteria for determining if a comment is nasty criticism meant to hurt, banter, or a bit of serious criticism that is designed to be helpful and constructive? There are several useful criteria, including questions such as: (1) who says it, (2) in what context, (3) how often, and (4) how many people. The

Talmudic quip is cute and serious at the same time, but not as nuanced as the version I heard in the 1970s. However, the bottom line is the same.

What is that bottom line? That human nature is such that we mostly dismiss critical comments, often to our detriment. It is beyond difficult to hear things that don't fit our rigid self-image. If we see ourselves as intelligent and kind, being called a donkey will surely not be received well. It will bring anger, denial (very possibly justified), and rejection. The question becomes, when does what someone says merit serious listening and self-examination, and when is it something to dismiss out of hand?

The nineteenth-century Musar movement, started by Rabbi Israel Lipkin of Salant (often called Rabbi Israel Salanter), was designed to help its followers work on their *midot*, or personal character traits. Disciples were trained to seek out opinions of teachers, colleagues, and friends to find ways to improve their character. It was unusual to be called a donkey, but disciples would very likely hear constructive suggestions on how levels of kindness, compassion, honesty, sincerity, and self-discipline could be raised. The recipients of such suggestions were trained to take them seriously. It was a mark of maturity, and even joy, to find new and better ways to improve personal character. All the better to serve God and other humans! But lacking that kind of intensive preparation, the average fallible human being is not ready to hear negative comments about his or her character.

The value of this Talmudic aphorism is that it furthers the kind of personal growth training that the Musar movement tried to institute in the nineteenth century. The more you get used to the idea that constructive, well-meant suggestions are valuable, the more ready your heart and mind are to receive them. It is also helpful to have an aphorism and an image. The aphorism is provided by this statement, and the image of the donkey and saddle may quickly come to mind when the question of useful feedback arises. The most optimistic outcome of repeating this dictum and seeing the image is that when you hear constructive criticism, you will be more emotionally ready to receive it, give it serious evaluation, and integrate the information into your personality. This is easier said than done, but it's a step in the right direction.

Once again the ancient Rabbis prove—through their teachings, and through their selection of popular, universal sayings—that their emotional intelligence was far ahead of their age. We twenty-first-century descendents would do well to take their advice to heart.

PRIVATE MORALITY

Whatever behavior the sages forbade
because of "appearance sake,"
is also forbidden in complete privacy.

Shabbat 146b

The sages were keen students of human nature, and of our pro-
clivities to moral failure. There are two levels (at least) of judging
human behavior, in their view. One is doing the right thing, and
the other is the appearance of doing the right thing.

I confess to being a bit surprised at the mention of the word
"appearances," *mar-it ayin,* in this statement. I suppose this is part
of the Rabbis' finely honed understanding of human habit and
normal interest. They start with the known and then go to the
unknown, as many good teachers will do. In this case, they also
start with the interesting, and then go to the less obvious.

We mortals, whether we admit it or not, are concerned with
how others perceive us. We do so many things simply because we
want to appear a certain way to others. This applies to the clothing we wear, our decorum, our attendance at meetings, the car we
drive, the home we live in, and a host of other important and
not-so-important preferences in life. The Rabbis were not insensitive to the fact that people like to be liked. Many statements in

rabbinic literature testify to their recognition of the human need for approval. So the Rabbis began with this premise and the reality that there needed to be a regulation (a moral law, even if it has no "teeth" or enforcement attached to it) regarding behavior that is public.

The Rabbis insisted that their followers behave in a way that would be *perceived* as moral and fitting. Moral and fitting, that is, for someone who is bound in covenant with a God who demands moral behavior from participants in the covenant.

In an unusual passage in the Talmud, the Rabbis make a distinction regarding immoral behavior by a rabbinic scholar when it is done publicly and fragrantly and when it is carried out in a private fashion. "Rav Ilai the Elder said: If a man sees that his evil urge is overwhelming him, let him go to a place where he is unknown, don black and cover himself with black, and do as his heart desires, but let him not publicly profane God's name" (Kiddushin 40a and Hagigah 16a).

It was clear to the sages that many mortal persons would on occasion commit some act that was a departure from acceptable norms—some acts worse than others. If it has to be so—and let it be known that they did not condone this behavior—then let it not be seen or known by others. The act is unacceptable in and of itself, but it is far worse if done in a way that lets others know about it, which would bring shame to the Jewish people, and thus to God. The statement we are studying is an ideal, and what Rav Ilai suggests is a failure to reach this ideal. But he seems to be arguing that there are degrees of failure.

Then the Rabbis moved to the next level. Is it enough to behave morally in public and not be concerned about what we do in private? Obviously not. In the *Shaharit* service we pray each day: "May one always revere God in private as in public" (*L'olam yehay adam y'ray shamayim ba-seter u'va-galui*). It's a bit like the question, does the tree make a sound when it falls in the forest and no one is there to hear it? While that is abstract philosophy, this is concrete morality.

There is also the issue of how we behave when we think no one is watching, but we still behave morally because we know that God is watching. Or, put another way, is there such a thing as "when no one is watching"? God knows what we're doing even if no one else does. So when we behave morally because God is watching, is that also "for the sake of appearance"? When God is watching, should our behavior be the same as it would be when humans are watching. Let's give ourselves the benefit of the doubt and assume that if we do something because no human being is watching, but because we know that God *is* watching, that is still a very high moral level. It implies that we care about being moral, even if on some level we feel that there will be consequences from up high, if not from down here.

Rabbinic morality is concerned with both public and private behavior. What is objectionable in front of others is also objectionable in front of no one. We should do the right thing because it is the right thing, and not only because of what others might think or say, or how they may or may not react. That is a higher level of ethics than is currently honored by many politicians and other public figures, and it ought to be the level that defines and dictates all of our actions.

THE GOLDEN RULE

**What is hateful to you
do not do to your neighbor!**

Shabbat 31a

There has been much ink spilled over the issue of whether the Golden Rule as it is often stated—Do unto your neighbor as you would have them do unto you—is more worthy than the way Hillel couched it in the Talmud, which is in the negative. Let's leave that discussion to you to figure out another time. The point is essentially the same. The Golden Rule sets up a standard regarding that which you yourself do not like. Essentially, your preferences, your likes and dislikes, and the effects that the behavior of others have on you become the standard by which you judge your own behavior toward others.

The standard is a relative one, and not a constant one. It depends on how you feel about something done to another person. The difficult part is that it may vary from individual to individual. But its strength lies in the fact that each person is usually pretty clear on what bothers him or her. You do not need to look up in a book what the standard is, or check with an expert. All you need to do is look inside yourself and decide what is comfortable for you and what is not. The simplicity, clarity, and certainty of this standard make it very usable and functional.

What are some of the things that might be "hateful to yourself"? No one wants others to steal from them, hurt them, be unfair to them, or berate them. So even though the standard seems relative and subjective, it turns out that human beings are mostly similar in their hearts, and what is hateful to one is usually hateful to all.

The benefit of making the individual the standard is that it inevitably raises the level of each person's moral standards. By not doing to others what is hateful to yourself, you will by definition end up behaving in ways that are generally considered decent, ethical, and just. If every human being followed this rule, our world would be a much better place. No one would steal, cheat, act disloyally, speak hurtfully, or gossip about or slander another person. By avoiding these common negative behaviors humanity would move a long way toward becoming more sensitive, compassionate, and caring. Not without reason is this referred to as the Golden Rule.

III

Personal Values through Humility, Awareness, and Dignity

"Your own conduct will command respect for you."

Tractate Eduyot 9b

THE POWER OF PEACE

**Great is peace
since peace is to the world
what leaven is to dough.**

Perek HaShalom, Midrash Vayikra Rabbah 9:9

I have always loved aphorisms. My son Jonathan and I translated some years ago a book called *Hasidic Wisdom*, compiled by Simcha Raz, that is full of the most wise and profound insights about life that anyone could imagine. The statement at hand, relating to the importance of peace, is one such aphorism—brief, insightful, eloquent, and relating a very important idea.

Peace is like motherhood and apple pie. Who could be against it? But the real meaning of peace is in the details. What kind of peace? Whose peace? Whose idea of peace? Peace at what cost? What does peace accomplish? Everyone (or almost everyone) wants peace—shalom/salaam—in the Middle East. But what will bring peace? What boundaries are necessary? What promises, commitments, and conditions must be in place? Will peace mean friendship, or just security? Will it involve an exchange of students, scientists, and diplomats, or just an absence of Katyusha rockets, homicide bombers, and other pernicious and relentless forms of terror? Peace, as we can see, is in the details.

Our statement from Perek HaShalom shouts out that peace is great. How so? It fills the role in the world the way leaven fills in dough. And what does leaven do for dough? It takes a quiet, useless glob of proteins and turns it into something useful, productive, and functional. It raises the dough from its natural flat state and gives it form, shape, and strength. In the metaphor of the Talmudic mind, the leaven is what creates passion in humans and gives us our emotions, our desires, our will to live. Were it not for this special passion, no one would procreate or build a house. It is the critical ingredient in the human personality and soul that turns on the switch of aliveness.

So it is with peace. Add this ingredient to the mix of people, land, selfishness, laziness, nationalism, self-defense, and a host of other emotions, circumstances, and other factors. See how it can turn a world of tension, conflict, and battle—one filled with waste, unhappiness, poverty, sickness, lack of productivity, and many other forms of dysfunction—into a thriving, exciting, enabling, and fruitful society.

The metaphor of leaven is often used in rabbinic literature. It bespeaks the effectiveness of language that the Talmudic sages employed to their (and our) great benefit. Let us dissect this metaphor a bit further. Leaven is an agent that, when added to other ingredients, is like a match that starts a blaze, or a key in a machine that creates combustion. This is the power that transforms something inert into something explosive and powerful.

What is the *nimshal*, or referent, in the case of peace? In one short sentence the Rabbis convey the notion that the magical power of peace turns on an engine, or sets fire to an idle furnace, which in turn provides heat, power, and function for its users. Peace can do that for the world. When conflict reigns, people's attention, resources, and energies are devoured by their need for self-protection. All creativity, positive use of talent, and human potential are spent on the pursuit of stability and safety. Little poetry is written, few paintings are spread across quiet, waiting canvasses, hardly any heart-rending music is written to serenade lovers or soothe the strain of hassled humanity. (There is, of course, the theory, borne out by such periods as Elizabethan England and others, that it is precisely in wartime that the creative muse is fired up the most.) Personally I believe that peacetime enables greater numbers of people to be more creative.

In other words, peace is the positive agent that functions as a catalyst to bring out the divine in human beings. War, conversely, brings out fear, anxiety, and defensiveness—not a spiritual or psychological condition that is conducive to higher-level functioning. The highest spiritual moments in our lives are those in which shalom, in its fullest sense of wholeness and completeness, enables God's creatures to live at their best.

Indeed, great is peace because it is the primary condition for living an inventive, imaginative, innovative, and exciting life, one filled with joy, purpose, anticipation, harmony, and the desire to reach for the sky.

COMMUNITY

**Whoever shares a congregation's grief
will merit to see its comfort and relief.**

Taanit 11a

This insightful aphorism asks an important question: are you a steadfast friend of the community, or are you a fair-weather friend? A steadfast friend is there in good times and in bad times, in days of anguish and anxiety as well as in days of abundance, prosperity, and success. It helps answer the questions: What constitutes membership in a community? Is the community like a service station that is available in times of need, regardless of what we do to support it?

A good comparison is a Sears store. Whether I need to go there to buy a toaster oven, bath towels, or a new flat-screen television, there are enough people who support the store that I don't need to worry about its viability between purchases. If the store falls in profits during one or more quarters, it has little effect on me (unless I own stock in the company). It is unlikely that the company's CEO will call upon me for assistance in promoting its products or in swaying people to frequent the store. The CEO won't seek my opinion about the design of its displays or about any other question that relates to its survivability. The store is there, and when I need it, I'll go there, and when I don't, I won't.

A community, on the other hand, is an organic body that needs to be nourished and supported by steadfast friends and people who truly care about its welfare. The community could be a small one, such as a *havurah,* a local chapter of B'nai B'rith, a Hadassah group, or a synagogue. Or it could be a large one—a neighborhood such as Great Neck or Monsey, New York, an organization like American Friends of Laniado Hospital in Netanya, Israel, a nationwide group of parents whose children live in Israel, or even the Jewish people as a whole.

The community I am most closely associated with is an American synagogue, so let's use that as an example. Any synagogue has its ups and downs. It has periods of growth in membership, sound budgetary health, successful staff appointments, congenial lay leadership, attractive programming, creative youth and adult education, and so on. It also has periods when all of these things are less than stellar. It could find itself in a changing neighborhood, in a financial climate in which its members have a hard time paying dues and fees for services, in a period when young members are not joining and the median age is rising, or in a quandary when a new, less demanding, synagogue has opened a modern, attractive building nearby, perhaps with a charismatic young rabbi who attracts many of the undecided unaffiliated in the area.

Some synagogues last for centuries; others find it necessary to sell their facility and merge with a nearby sister-congregation, with its assets such as *Sifray Torah* and stained-glass windows going to the larger, successful "takeover" congregation.

What the Talmud is saying is that any such community will succeed insofar as its members have built a reservoir of loyalty, memories, and warm, positive associations, so that in troubled times they will do everything in their power to marshal the financial, psychological, and other resources to keep it afloat. If the members care deeply about the community or institution and are willing to share the down times, they will likely also see it rise again, phoenix-like, from the ashes of despair to the mountain peaks of joy, celebration, and success.

Nothing comes without a price. The price of a successful community is the willingness of its constituents to see it through grief to relief, from illness to health. Any community with such members is fortunate indeed and will ultimately see a positive result and reward for its devoted efforts.

FAIRNESS IN JUDGMENT

**Every judge should see himself
as though a sword is about to enter his body,
and hell is open at his feet.**

Sanhedrin 7b

If anything, Judaism is a system of truth, fairness, and integrity. If we were to open a biblical concordance and look for words like justice, honesty, and equality, we would no doubt find many hundreds of references. Justice in the Jewish court system is demanded over and over again, and no influence, bribe, or favoritism is ever allowed to enter into the equation of dispensing fair and honest judgment.

The demand for strict justice in the ancient world is not something we should take for granted. There was no system of checks and balances, no brakes on the passion of the judge/king, no external criteria of abstract ideals, and no divine imperatives demanding equal treatment for all—that is, not until the appearance of the Torah. Codes of law existed in ancient Mesopotamia, but they were based on what was utilitarian, and not on any religious philosophic notion of right and wrong. A defendant was more often than not at the whim of a capricious system ruled by a capricious, mortal human whose primary interest was his own welfare. Along came the Torah, positing an overarching notion of justice that God built into the world. Nothing like this had ever been known before. It was a revolution that changed the world and society forever.

A person's right of appeal, based on a divine book that was given by the God of Justice for all people, of all nations, races, and ethnic backgrounds, was unheard of. The ability to argue with God, as Abraham did in the case of Sodom and Gomorrah, and to appeal to a "Judge of all the Earth" (Genesis 18:25) was unprecedented.

The system of higher and lower courts that was suggested by Jethro, father-in-law of Moses, set up a template for the judicial system that evolved into a fair, democratic society. In later, Talmudic times, when the Great Sanhedrin was established, justice was even more carefully dispensed, along with many books of rules and laws (Mishnah, Talmud, etc.) that ensured the permanent nature of a just society. This carefully crafted legal system became firmly entrenched in Israelite society as century followed century. The biblical prophets Isaiah, Amos, Micah, and others contributed no small share of moral background in their eloquent preaching about the need for a fair, just, and compassionate society.

This biblical background contributed to the atmosphere in which the Rabbis could utter a statement like the one we are examining—that a judge should feel as though a sword would pierce his heart, or he would jump over the abyss into hell, if he handed down an inequitable decision. The power and eloquence of these metaphors are typical of the pedagogic use of hyperbole by the Rabbis in their effective conveyance of Torah.

But we need not limit the implications of this teaching to the system of courts and judges. We descendants of the Pharisees have the right to create our own midrash on the ancient texts and to see in them more than their composers saw. Who in life does not, at some time or another, have to pass judgment on the

well-being of another, sometimes in serious matters and sometimes in less weighty ones? Nevertheless we are all judges at different times in our lives.

How would it influence our judgments if we imagined a sword
pointed at our heart? Or a hole next to our foot into which we
would fall to hell were our judgment harmful? The world would
be a better place if every judge (really, all of us) would use such
care and discretion when passing judgment on another.

Maybe every professional judge should include in his or her
oath of office a pledge to fall on a sword, or to jump into hell, if
any decision perverts the divine standards of fairness that he or
she has committed to uphold. And maybe all human beings
should visualize this imagery when exercising judgment that
affects the future of another child of God.

HUMILITY

One should constantly learn from the Creator.
The Holy Blessed One disregarded high mountains
and lofty hills,
and made visible the Divine Presence on lowly Mount Sinai.
Likewise God disdained all the majestic trees,
and brought forth the Divine Presence
in a lowly Burning Bush.

Sotah 5a

As saintly and pious role models of a holy life, the Talmudic
Rabbis stressed many personal qualities that led to the kind of life
they held up as their ideal. Such humanistic values as integrity,
commitment, service, perseverance, compassion, and loyalty were
stressed in their abundant writings. Among the many *midot*, or
character traits, they frequently heralded was humility.

In Pirke Avot we find many aphorisms that lionize the humble
person, following the precedents of verses in Psalms and other
places in the Tanakh.

What is characteristic of these gifted teachers is their ability to
use known metaphors to help their disciples emblazon such values into their moral consciousness. At the same time, they

wanted to hang their ideals on the pegs of biblical scenes and well-known historical events in Jewish tradition. By referencing Mount Sinai and the Burning Bush, they nailed their message hard and fast to the learner, creating a lesson that would not soon be forgotten.

It is not totally clear why the Rabbis believed that Sinai was a low mountain. Perhaps because Moses was able to climb the mountain to the top, and may not have been able to do so with some of the other mountains in the region—a region the Rabbis knew from their own travels, or tales of the travels of others. In any case, they deemed Mount Sinai one of the lower hills in the Sinai desert.

In the case of the Burning Bush it is easier to understand how they conceived of a lowly growth in nature, when God could have appeared to Moses at the beginning of Exodus from a high and mighty tree. A bush by definition is not an expansive natural phenomenon, but rather a simple, small, humble creation.

Thus, the two major visible manifestations of God to Moses and the People of Israel took place in modest, natural scenes in nature rather than in stately and majestic settings. A moral lesson can be found here, concluded the Rabbis. If God chose Mount Sinai and an unnamed out-of-the-way bush as places to convey some of the most important divine messages (the Ten Commandments and the call to Moses to be God's redeeming prophet), there must be a reason. They concluded that things of small size and stature may contain some of our most valuable moral teachings. If this is true of God's appearances to people, it must also be true of God's creatures, who are human as well.

Why stress humility? If we want to understand the importance of humility, it is necessary to look at its opposite traits—arrogance, egotism, and condescension. Surely these are some of the causes of the world's major problems, including the flaws found in most of God's sentient creatures. Who can deny that heinous things that occur in interpersonal relationships—in crises in the family, friendship, community, and indeed in the entire world—are often the result of arrogance and haughtiness?

When one person or group dominates another, it does not make for a harmonious or amicable relationship. It is also inevitable that opinions and ideas about small and large matters will bump up against each other in every couple, every friendship, and every area of discussion and negotiation. How these potential ruptures and tensions are dealt with is mostly dependent on the ability of each side to step back and see the other's point of view. To assume that the truth is not wholly yours, and that it is necessary to make room for the ideas of others, even when you are thoroughly convinced of your righteousness, is a trait of the humble, not the arrogant. A humble person makes room for others. A haughty individual, society, or nation pushes others out of the way, which may ultimately lead to a verbal or physical explosion.

Humility serves another very important role in the human personality. It allows for a sense of awe and reverence. It makes room for an understanding of the world as a place that is divine in origin and unique in design.

For these reasons the Rabbis embraced humility and tried to find ways, including biblical references like Mount Sinai and the Burning Bush, to bring home their important message that arrogance and egotism destroy, and humility brings harmony and peace.

CHOOSE TO BE PERSECUTED RATHER THAN PERSECUTE ANOTHER

One should always be among those who are persecuted, rather than among those who persecute.

Bava Kama 93a

The Jewish people has a long history of being persecuted. One tradition says that anti-Semitism began at Mount Sinai when the Jews received the Torah. The play on words in Hebrew is that *sinah* (hatred) came from Sinai. This might mean that people have hated the Jews because of their high moral standards dictated in the Torah. Or it might mean that *sinah* began at the earliest stages of Jewish peoplehood.

The Jews were chased, persecuted, exiled, and vilified during their forty years of wandering in the Sinai desert by the Midianites, Amalekites, Ammonites, and others; they were later attacked by the Assyrians, Babylonians, Greeks, Romans, and many other nations all through history. Anti-Semitism, according to Menachem Begin, the late prime minister of Israel, passes down through the mother's milk of Israel's enemies.

Against this historical background we read the stern admonishment of the sages that it is preferable to be persecuted than to be among those who persecute. The statement by itself is on a high ethical plane. To ask people to choose being a victim rather than an attacker is an audacious stance. Add to that a long history of persecution—the knowledge and personal experience of pain, anguish, and frustration at being mistreated—and asking someone to swallow that dose of misery, and to rise above it, is truly a remarkable level of ethical expectation.

It is interesting to note that the Rabbis postulate two polarities. In the course of existence, people sometimes have cause to be rough and tough and militant, either for self-defense or to establish their position in society or among nations. Likewise people have cause to be passive and let the other side win, pour out wrath, or behave militantly; the passive person sits back and just takes it, in the interest of letting things pass. This is choosing your battles, so to speak. In reality we do not have the life choice to be the persecutor or the one persecuted. All of us, to a degree, may sometimes be tough and other times soft. But if given the choice, and if there is a polarity, say the sages, then be among those who are on the receiving end of hatred, wickedness, pogroms, violence, and attack, rather than among those who dish out this nastiness to others.

If we think of situations in which a person is chased (*nirdaf* in Hebrew), we could come up with many possibilities—a store robbery, ethnic or religious discrimination, violent states of affairs such as terrorism or even war, and so on. In each such situation, our behavior may be different and have a different ethical valence, depending on who is the pursuer and why.

By making a general statement that covers a multitude of circumstances, the Rabbis are surely conjuring up their historical memories of being driven out of their homes and/or homeland and saying to their disciples, "Don't ever let yourself be found in the position of the wicked Romans or Greeks, who denied us our dignity, our rights, our humanness, and sometimes our very lives. It is better to be beaten, perhaps even to die, than to turn into a monster of a human being."

The Rabbis are prepared to suffer the worst consequences, to put themselves in the most compromising positions of danger and insecurity, than to act in ways that go against the deepest grain of ethical behavior, and the high norms of proper treatment of another.

FLEXIBILITY

**One should always be as flexible as a reed;
and not be rigid as a cedar.**

Taanit 20

This bit of wisdom is the result of an interesting experience related in the Talmud, as follows:

> A story is told of Rabbi Elazar son of Rabbi Simeon, who was once returning from his teacher's house in Migdal Eder. He was riding leisurely on his donkey by the lakes and felt thoroughly satisfied with himself because he had studied much Torah. He then came upon a very ugly man who greeted him by saying, "Peace be upon you, my master." Rabbi Elazar did not return the greeting but instead said to him, "You worthless creature! How ugly you are! Are all the people of your city as ugly as you?"
>
> The man replied, "What can I do about it? Go tell the Craftsman who made me, 'How ugly is the vessel You have made!'" No sooner did Rabbi Elazar realize that he had done wrong than he got down from the donkey and, prostrating himself before the man, said to him, "I apologize to you. Please forgive me!"

The man replied, "I will not forgive you until you go to the Craftsman who made me and say, 'How ugly is the vessel You have made!'"

Rabbi Elazar followed him until he reached the man's city. When the people of the city came out to meet Rabbi Elazar, greeting him with the words "Peace be upon you, my master, my teacher," the man asked them, "Whom are you addressing as 'My master, my teacher'?"

They replied, "The man who is walking behind you." At that, the man said, "If he is the master, may there be no more like him in Israel!" When the people asked him why, he replied, "This is how this man behaved toward me." They said to him, "Nevertheless, forgive him, for he is greatly learned in Torah."

The man replied, "For your sakes, I forgive him, but only on condition that he not make a habit of such behavior."

Rabbi Elazar son of Rabbi Simeon immediately entered the *bet midrash* and lectured on the subject "One should at all times be pliant as a reed and not hard as a cedar" (Taanit 20).

Often the most important lessons in life emerge from personal experience. Not everyone, of course, learns from experience. Many people repeat their mistakes over and over again. Habit is a harsh taskmaster. What is noteworthy about this story is that Rabbi Elazar was able to rise above his foolish arrogance and recognize the flaw that was in himself. Not only that, but he then made a public example of his flaw by lecturing on the subject and creating a saying that others could repeat—one that would remind them of the lesson and, by force, the story attached to it. What a courageous and brave act he performed!

The difference between a fool and a sage is not that a fool makes mistakes and a sage never does. All of us make mistakes.

We are all mortal, frail, fallible creatures of bad habits and with character flaws. The difference between a fool and a sage is that the sage recognizes mistakes, learns from them, corrects them, and moves beyond them. A fool repeats them again and again.

The specific lesson here is that a person should never be too arrogant to admit a mistake, and even to beg forgiveness from another. Rabbi Elazar does not fall in our estimation by doing these things. On the contrary, as we watch his sense of decency overcome his evil inclination, our opinion of him becomes more favorable. Arrogance is a characteristic of many great people. It is very difficult not to feel smug and self-satisfied when reaching great achievements. As a renowned Torah scholar, Rabbi Elazar was feeling very proud of himself. Forgetting that the essence of Torah is humility, he let out a haughty comment that he should have kept to himself. He quickly realized his mistake and apologized. Therein lies his greatness and the source of our admiration. His lesson is one that other generations can repeat so that we can all aspire to reach his level of sagacity and to be as flexible and humble as he turned out to be.

LIVING IN THE NOW

**Worry yourself not about tomorrow
lest there be no tomorrow.
And it turns out that you are worried
about a world that is not yours.**

Sanhedrin 100b

Many profound sayings are easier said than done. This proverb resembles dozens of others that remind people not to waste too much time fretting about the future or the past, but rather to try to live in the present. It is one of the most important pieces of philosophical and psychological guidance that exists. It is also one of the most difficult to carry out.

The late Frederic (Fritz) Perls, founder of the Gestalt therapy movement, believed that all neuroses stem from not living in the present. We worry too much about what might happen, and we regret too often the things we might have done. We bury ourselves in the future or in the past.

In my collection of quotations, *Moments of the Spirit: Quotations to Inspire, Inform and Involve,* there is the following:

> To remember the past, to live in the present, and to trust in the future (Abba Kovner).

Some there are that torment themselves afresh with the memory of what is past; others again, afflict themselves with the apprehensions of evils to come. The one does not now concern us, and the other not yet. One should count each day a separate life (Seneca).

God's miracles belong to those who can concentrate on one thing and limit themselves (Baal Shem Tov).

My friend and colleague Rabbi Jack Riemer examines a passage in the biblical Book of Exodus about which he wrote to me:

Near the end of [the] Torah Reading [Mishpatim] there appears a strange verse. God says to Moses, "*Aley hahara, vihey sham*, Go up to the top of the mountain, and *be there*." Do you feel the strangeness of that expression? Would it not have been enough for God to say to Moses to go up to the top of the mountain? Why does God tell Moses, not only to go up to the top of the mountain, but also to *be there*?

The [Hasidic rebbe known as the] Kotsker looked at this passage in this week's sidrah, the one in which God tells Moses to not only go up the mountain, but also to *be* there, and he says that what it means is that it is easy to climb up the mountain, anyone can do that. The real task and the real test of the religious person is to stay there, to stand there, to remain focused there, and not to be distracted away from the meaning of this place and this moment. What God was saying to Moses, according to the Kotsker, was that it is not enough to have a brief and exciting spiritual experience, and then go on to something else. The real challenge is to hold on to the moment, to be in the moment, to not be distracted away from the moment.

I started by saying that living in the now is one of the easiest things to advise but one of the most difficult things to do. I have been teaching this idea for decades and I must confess that I still have a lot of trouble focusing on one thing at a time. My mind has a tendency to wander. I am easily distracted and my thoughts meander often. But perhaps people like me are what motivated this Talmudic saying. So many of us think too much about the future instead of enjoying the moment. Nevertheless it is worth trying to do, even though it might be an ideal that is never completely achieved.

To round out the rabbinic wisdom of this chapter, I offer readers the advice of two important Hasidic teachers. First, Rabbi Mordechai of Lechovitz wrote that "All worrying is forbidden, except to worry that one is worried." And second, Rabbi Yehiel of Zlotchov taught the following:

> There are two things it is forbidden to worry about:
> That which it is possible to fix,
> And that which it is impossible to fix.
> What is possible to fix—fix it, and why worry?
> What is impossible to fix—how will worrying help?

Enough said.

Self-Reliance and
Human Dignity

**Rather make your Shabbat like a day of the week,
than depend on the help of others.**

Pesachim 112a

A bit of background is necessary to understand the full weight of this proverb. While some modern Jews still focus their whole life around Shabbat, it is not nearly as commonly observed as it was in Talmudic times. In those days, Shabbat was truly the center of the universe of the Jew. Preparation for Shabbat took place all week long. As soon as Shabbat was over on Saturday night, the family would begin to prepare for the next Shabbat. The best food, the most special tableware, the finest clothing—all of this was set aside for Shabbat. Most Jews lived fairly simple lives, and Shabbat was a respite from labor, from the struggles of life that came from persecution, and from the battles to get from one day to the next.

Throughout Jewish history Shabbat was an island of peace, serenity, and physical and spiritual relaxation in the Jewish home. It was the day that most resembled the "days of the Messiah." For that reason, at the end of Shabbat, we sing of Elijah, the prophet who was the precursor of the Messiah. It is impossible to exaggerate the importance of Shabbat in the life of the average Jew—the tranquility, fulfillment, and life-giving quality it added to the humdrum existence of the rest of the week.

Thus, it is easier to understand the significance of what this advice implies. To make Shabbat "like a day of the week" would have been a major sacrifice to the traditional Jew.

This was a time when the biggest outlay of money was dedicated to the enhancement of Shabbat—for a nicer meal, for a larger portion of food, for a higher quality of meat for the main course, or for a special dessert. If funds were not available, it would be natural to think of taking a small loan from a close relative or friend to tide the family over for a few days so that Shabbat would be distinctive and truly a day set apart from the rest of the week. Most of us would not consider it a terrible thing, if we were struggling financially and needed a small loan for a very important cause, to turn to someone who would help us and not let it be known to others what our difficulty was.

And yet, this Talmudic advice stresses the value of self-reliance and independence, even above the tradition of enhancing Shabbat meals. The dignity and self-respect that could be compromised by turning to another for even a small amount of money is too precious to risk, even for the increased joy of a Shabbat celebration.

Celebrating Shabbat is a very important value, and Shabbat observance, in the fullest sense, is what has sustained the Jewish people spiritually throughout its history. However, the teacher in this case makes it clear that not even Shabbat trumps the importance of human dignity, pride, honor, and self-reliance. As important as ritual, Shabbat, and the festivals are, they never transcend the human values they seek to promote.

THE VALUE OF
PHYSICAL LABOR

**Greater is one who enjoys physical labor,
than one who is pious and idle.**

Berakhot 8a

In Talmudic times everyone was involved in physical labor, even rabbis. Long before the information age, when people are now paid for their knowledge (authors, lawyers, physicians, clergy, consultants, and so on), the only way to make a living was through the sweat of our brow. There were shoemakers, farmers, shepherds, vintners, and shopkeepers. The Rabbis read the first half of Exodus 20:9, "six days you will labor," as a separate injunction and not merely as an introduction to the prohibition of work on Shabbat.

Rabbi Yehudah HaNasi said, "these words constitute a separate commandment. Just as the people of Israel was commanded concerning Shabbat, so were they commanded concerning work" (Midrash, Bereshit Rabbah 16:8). In another passage, this hyperbolic demand was articulated: "One who does not teach a child a trade is as though the child were taught to be a robber" (Kiddushin 29a). This was not the universal view, as some scholars thought studying every waking hour was the supreme good. But such a view was not held by the majority.

This proverb makes an interesting and noteworthy point. It is based on a scriptural anomaly that states, "Happy are those who fear Adonai. [But if] you enjoy the fruit of your labors, you shall have [a double blessing] of happiness and well-being" (Psalm 128:1–2).

Conventional wisdom teaches that piety, or fear of heaven, is almost an unmatched ideal. God is our creator, redeemer, and teacher. Respect, awe, and honor to God is, as William Shakespeare wrote, a "consummation devoutly to be wished." The major activities of Jewish religious life are centered around God: praying to God, study of God's Torah, and care for God's children through tzedakah and *gemilut hasadim* (acts of lovingkindness). You would think that fearing God is the *summum bonum*, the supreme good from which all else is derived.

The proverb presents an unexpected and counterintuitive viewpoint, as do so many rabbinic statements and teachings. This surprise element is one of the ways the Rabbis seize our attention and communicate an important point. Perhaps they exaggerated and did not intend to convey the full meaning of their saying. Nevertheless, by saying the opposite of what we might believe, they stressed a value that might otherwise be neglected.

In this case, I believe the Rabbis were trying to emphasize that physical labor is not to be scorned. Nor is it a dispensable necessity that, were we so fortunate to be born into wealth, we should avoid like the plague. The belief in the value of manual labor was strong among many rabbinic teachers. Some felt that a person who engages in manual labor surpasses in the value hierarchy even a God-fearing person who is without such work. Getting our hands dirty in the daily business of self-sustenance is an honorable and necessary part of being human, and no one dare make light of it.

The dialogue between those who see spiritual activity alone as sufficient and those who believe that we must also engage in the daily nitty-gritty responsibilities of caring for home, community, and country continues in many forms. In the State of Israel even today there are those who think that studying in a yeshivah is a reasonable excuse for not serving in the military. Other Orthodox leaders have created a special kind of yeshivah, known as a Hesder Yeshivah, in which young people alternate between devoting their time to military service and Torah study. Many secular Israelis feel that anyone who avoids military service by matriculating in a yeshivah is derelict in his or her duty to the nation. This conflict is the source of much passionate debate and burning rancor in Israel.

The Rabbis did not have to go as far as they did in elevating physical work above even pious beliefs and behavior. They may have expressed it in this form to make a point through hyperbole. Or, it is possible that the teacher who made this statement truly believes that hands-on involvement in subsistence is so basic to human life that it comes before ethereal pursuits such as study and prayer. In either case, it is clear that the intention here was to push the pendulum in the other direction from those who argue that fear of God and doing the things we normally associate with the life of the spirit are the very highest level that anyone can achieve. Instead, he argues, the work of making the world go around includes both the spiritual and the material, and no one should think that either is, or ever will be, dispensable.

IV

Family Values: Living Respectfully with Mates, Children, and Parents

"One who teaches Torah to children abides with the divine presence."

Bava Metzia 85

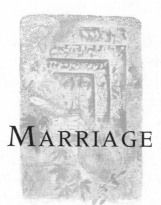

MARRIAGE

**Matching a man and woman in marriage
is as difficult as splitting the Reed Sea.**

Sotah 2a

The Rabbis were realistic in the extreme. We might even say that their views on relationships, human weakness, values, ideals, and aspirations were ahead of their time, and rarely bashful or reserved. They were guilty neither of some of the strict Victorian attitudes we see in contemporary society nor of the vulgar excesses that bombard us through the media. They faced life in all its boldness, harshness, and immaturities. What you see is what they saw, described, and expressed.

In any bookstore today you will find scores of books on having a good marriage, with romantic and Pollyannaish descriptions of the ideal relationship. But the Rabbis are saying that it is not easy to find a mate, and by extension, to maintain a good relationship with a spouse.

Witness today the multitude of dating sites on the Internet. In the old days, there was a *shadchan* (matchmaker), like in *Fiddler on the Roof*, who knew all the local boys and girls—which is what they were in those times, since marriage took place when the bride and groom were in their teens—and made the best matches possible. Today, when people can cross the country, and even national borders, to find a mate, we could say that it is easier—or harder—to explore the compatibility of a prospective life partner.

We are really talking about two processes. One is finding the right mate and the other is keeping the relationship going. Neither is easy. Today there are many people who feel that finding the right person is so important that they experiment for years, sometimes decades, until they think they are certain. And with making a commitment being such a difficult and frightening thing today, all too many singles make a virtue out of a necessity and remain unattached for life.

Some people believe, like the Rabbis, that marriages in the old days were just as hard to make and keep as they are now, but back then people were less likely to end a relationship that was sanctified under the chuppah (wedding canopy) than they are today. In the 1960s, which is when the divorce rate began to climb, it became much more socially acceptable to end a marriage if one or both parties were unhappy. Recently, however, people have begun to return to the notion of commitment, of sticking it out, in sickness and in health, than what we saw in the latter part of the twentieth century.

Are the Rabbis suggesting that people should find a life partner and, even if the person is not perfect, take the plunge? Is that implied in their analysis? It is hard to tell, but given that they lived in a society in which divorce did not happen very often, that may very well have been on their minds. Maybe what they are teaching is that we should not expect to find the perfect partner, first, because no one is perfect, and second, because all relationships are difficult. Perhaps they are also teaching that since making the right match is far from easy, keeping it is equally difficult, so we should accept the less-than-perfect nature of such relationships and work on them as best we can.

Modern psychologists and marriage counselors would advise, I think, that when you are in a committed relationship, you should not expect smooth sailing. There is no couple that lacks disagreements, stylistic differences, and value conflicts, all of which occur in the normal course of a close relationship. That being the case, we should try to bring out the best in our partners, accept them as they are, and enjoy the good times. Otherwise, we can easily drown in misery. Divorce is an option in our tradition, but it is never a pleasant one, and it is especially painful when children are involved. So often it is more worthwhile to work hard to make it work. Not always, but often.

The somewhat harsh realism of the Rabbis is grounding in a world without moorings, without strong commitments, and without a clear sense of the sanctity of family life.

CARING FOR YOUR SPOUSE

**One should always be careful
not to hurt one's wife,
because her tears are ready
and she is easily hurt.**

Bava Metzia 59a

This reflection of the sages about dealing with your wife is at once compassionate and paternalistic. We feel the pathos and tenderness of a caring husband echo through these words. At the same time, we recognize the paternalism that is hidden behind the love, one that is understandable for its time.

It is more useful if our commentary on this aphorism takes the form of a modern midrash and examines the higher impulses and noble sentiments underlying the expression of caring. Thus, let us approach it from the point of view of the care anyone should take in dealing with a family member, close friend, or mate—male or female. An up-to-date translation would then be: We should always be careful not to hurt our dear one, or spouse, because we are most hurt by those closest to us.

Viewed from this modern, egalitarian viewpoint, we can gain much from this Talmudic saying.

Let's contextualize the statement by looking at relationships in general. It is conventional wisdom that we all take for granted our closest relationships, and thus can often be most frank with those whom we love the most. Our thinking is, the relationship is solid and almost nothing will destroy it. Given that assumption, we often allow ourselves to do and say things that are careless, hurtful, and insensitive. In our impatience, busyness, and smugness, we do not afford to our dearest friends and family the same cordiality and respect we do to those who are further away in intimacy.

What we need to do in relation to those nearest and dearest to us is say to ourselves, before speaking or acting, "Pretend that this is a stranger." Would we speak to a stranger the way we sometimes speak to those whom we love the most? In taking our loved ones for granted, we speak to them in a way we would never speak to someone less close to us. That is the problem with communication in intimate relationships.

We have high expectations of our loved ones, especially our spouse. We are often disappointed when these expectations are not met. Further, we are easily angered at our spouse due to miscommunication, unmet needs, and a variety of other reasons. When this happens, we have to work on developing patience, acceptance, and self-control. We know that we cannot expect our spouse to re-make him/herself in the image we had when we were married. That was an idealized picture of someone we thought we knew. We do not really know our partner until years pass and more of who we really are is revealed. The good qualities we loved when we developed the relationship are still there, but, of course, no one is perfect. And when we see things we were not aware of, our disappointment rises and our anger is kindled.

It is at that point that it helps to picture in our mind's eye the image of the person we love, instead of the person who is temporarily disappointing us. This visualization technique can go a long way in helping us develop patience and compassion, and transforming annoyance into affection and caring. As we glare into the face of our dearest one, we need to remember the thoughts and feelings we had when we first pledged loyalty and affection to our mate—the warm thoughts and loving and tender feelings that brought us together in the first place. That will change our attitude very quickly. Take a deep breath before expressing anger, frustration, or sarcasm. Let that image of deep love overcome any negative thoughts or ideas that may have arisen.

In the final analysis it is those we love to whom we owe the greatest debt of caring and attention. It is our mate to whom we owe the greatest commitment, and on whom we rely the most when things get rough, or when we want to share our greatest joys. Thus, the Rabbis teach us that we must go out of our way to treat our loved ones with the most gentle, patient, caring, and loving words and deeds available.

HONORING PARENTS

There are three partners in the making of a human being:
The Holy Blessed One, one's father and one's mother.
When people honor their parents
the Holy Blessed One credits them
as if God's Presence were among them
because they are honoring God!

Kiddushin 30b

Martin Buber, whose grandfather was a masterful scholar of
midrash and who surely influenced young Martin in the ways of
the human soul, drew upon this kind of Talmudic and Hasidic
humanism in his definition of God as existing in the narrow
bridge between human beings. God is in relationships! Perhaps
God is also in ashrams and yoga studios and mountain caves, as
well as in Reform, Conservative, and Orthodox synagogues. But
mostly God is in the relationships we have with those we love
and care deeply about.

If God is in all authentic, loving relationships, how much more
so is the Almighty part of the sacred bond forged with our parents. There are easily a hundred quotations that reflect the high
station in which the Rabbis held mothers and fathers, all of

which, of course, go back to the primal command in the Ten Words—that is, Ten Commandments—in the Torah (Exodus chapter 20; Deuteronomy chapter 5) to honor our father and mother.

Two issues arise when thinking about this Talmudic statement. First, what does it mean to honor our parents? Second, how does this act of honoring our mother and father exhibit a dimension of divinity?

To address the first question, there can surely be no boiler-plate definition of honor, for parents or anyone else. But we can grasp at some fundamental ideas without being overly definitive. Does honoring parents mean obeying them? In some part yes, depending on age and circumstances. More importantly, I would guess, it means performing acts of kindness and deference. Furthermore, I believe that honoring our parents embraces two components—an emotional one and an active one. The first is more difficult because it is problematical, if not impossible, to command or mandate how a person should feel. When the first paragraph of the *Shema* orders us to "Love Adonai our God," the commentators mainly see this as a command directed toward action, not emotion. The same concept holds here.

And yet, it is not unreasonable to ask of people, on a feeling level, to remember that it is our parents who bestowed the sacred gift of life on us, and that it is their genes we carry, for good or bad. It is they, moreover, who nurtured us as helpless infants, picked us up and comforted us when we cried, fed us when we were seized by the instinct of thirst or hunger, protected us from cold and danger, and helped heal our hurts and wounds in the painful years of maturation.

How can we repay such incalculable debts? Through acts of honor—deeds of thoughtfulness, respect, and kindheartedness.

To address the second question, what does God really want of the creatures who owe their lives not only to their parents but also to the third partner in the creation of a person—our Master and Maker? Does God want recitation of formulas, mechanical performance of rituals, and structured behaviors as laid out in codes of law? The Jewish answer to that question is decidedly yes. Ritual is inextricably bound with ethics in the Jewish tradition, but that is for another discussion. The point here is that God wants heart.

Rahamana liba ba-ay, says the Talmud: God desires heart. God desires warm affection and a pure soul—surely more than the pre-ordained performance of rites and sacraments, as important as these may be in sustaining the love of tradition and the continuity of our heritage. And if this is what God truly wants, then the best way to honor God is to honor all who are God's children. Among our human family, who can deny that our parents deserve the highest honor available?

FINANCES AND FAMILY

**When the barley is gone from the pitcher,
strife comes knocking at the door.**

Bava Metzia 59a

When I was a very young groom of twenty-two, someone gave me this advice: Be careful in dealing with your spouse when discussing two important matters—money and children. These are the things that cause the most fights.

Forty-five years and two marriages later, I can confirm the wisdom of this advice. Couples have differences of opinion on many matters, but conflicts over child-rearing and how to spend money are the two most frequent sources of argument. And it does not seem to matter whether a couple is rich or poor; the fights still seem, from what I have learned as a marriage counselor and from personal experience, to stem from these two areas.

Money has a symbolic power that overrules rationality. It represents independence, power, authority, control, security, and a host of other emotional dynamics. We all know people who work themselves to the bone to build up a large nest egg at the expense of time with their family. These people never seem to realize that the price for doing so is greater than all the money in the world.

The late Senator Paul Tsongas of Massachusetts once said that no one on his deathbed ever regretted not having spent more time at the office. How wise!

Even as far back as the rabbinic period it was understood that families quarrel most over financial (material) security. This statement, translated into modern psychological parlance, is that a lack of food results in anger. But it is clear that the aphorism covers problems much broader than the absence of food on the table. When spending has to be scrutinized because there is not enough money to go around, the values of different family members rise to the surface. That in turn leads to differences in opinion and conflicts of values. One thing leads to another and any suppressed anger bubbles to the surface. Every time one family member buys something that another thinks is unnecessary, the memory is stored as fodder for resentment. Every time someone buys a product that could have been bought at a less expensive store, or in a scaled-down version, there is the potential for a conflagration, large or small.

Then there is the whole issue of family inheritance and the dispensing of assets from parents and other relatives. How often have I and my rabbinic colleagues officiated at funerals at which the siblings would not speak to each other because of how much money or property was bequeathed to one child instead of the other? It's a story that plays out over and over and causes terrible discord in families that sometimes lasts for generations. It seems that money in these cases is a stand-in for affection, and siblings are always jealous of the affections of parents.

The Rabbis, in their statement, were alluding to an issue that has wide ramifications. The stress of unpaid bills, the pressure of a materialistic society that causes people to go deeper into debt so that they can keep up with their neighbors, and the insatiable desire people have for more "things" are extensions of a human trait that can be traced back for millennia. With the rising cost of health care, education, and housing, it makes it even more important for people to curb their lust for luxury, and distinguish between wants and needs.

INFLUENCE OF THE HOME

**Whatever youth say in the marketplace
comes from the home.**

Sukkah 56b

The influence of the family and the home on children's behavior is beyond measure. There are so many aphorisms that attest to this ancient truth—the apple does not fall far from the tree, and so on. Surely that is one reason Judaism places such strong emphasis on the home and family. Even more than the school and the synagogue, the home is where children learn their moral ABCs.

Jewish ethics stress the great obligations that parents have in raising children, starting with the Torah. "And you shall teach them diligently" (Deuteronomy 6:7), "Train a child in the way she should go, and she will not depart from it" (Proverbs 22:6), and so on. Schools came later in Jewish life. It is crucial for the home to reinforce what is taught in the school.

My late teacher Rabbi Mordecai Kaplan would often say that trying to teach youth without reinforcement at home is like attempting to heat a house while leaving all the windows open. This metaphor masterfully conveys the idea that the school and the home must be partners for successful moral and intellectual maturation to occur in our young people. And it was Nobel Peace

Prize winner Albert Schweitzer who said that there are three effective methods in teaching: by example, by example, and by example.

What are the things we ordinarily expect of parents, or of others who raise children? We hope that they impart a set of values, a core of behaviors that will stand their children in good stead throughout their lives. Society assumes that young people will learn the meaning of responsibility, compassion, sharing, integrity, and discipline, among other things. We also hope that they will learn the joy of experiencing life with other people. We pray that intimacy will be the gift of a few good friends, modeled by the relationship of mother and father. As Jews, we want our children to embrace, in addition to the universal human values that most parents transmit to their kids, their culture and tradition, and to be proud, committed, knowledgeable, and practicing Jews (on whatever level each family chooses for itself).

Am I overstating the power of parental influence? I don't think so. As years pass and I remember more (not less, ironically) of what my late mother and father, of blessed memory, were like, what norms and principles they lived by, I find that I am so similar to them in many ways. I wish they could somehow know that. And I see in my own adult children many of my own, and my parents', traits. It's almost as if we are locked into a series of forces that are beyond our control. But not entirely. I have surpassed my parents in a lot of ways, and I probably will never reach the greatness and specialness that my imagination attributes to them. My sense of humor, my shyness, my chutzpah, my compassion for suffering humanity, my generosity, my fears and anxieties—all these and more stem from what I saw, felt, and heard when I was growing up.

How often do I find myself saying, "My father used to say," or, "My mother would think this or that about such and such"? And how often do old friends and members of my family who knew my parents tell me how much I am like them in one way or another? Or how often do I think in my head that I am in some ways just a clone of my progenitors?

All of this is not to deny the power of people to overcome the negative parts of their background, or to suggest that we are guaranteed all the wonderful traits our creators possessed. We live our own lives, to be sure, and must take full responsibility for our choices, actions, and values. But the influence our parents have on our lives is so amazingly powerful that it would be foolish to deny its lasting impact.

And so the lesson is that the good parts of ourselves that we are lucky enough to possess must also be handed down to a new owner in mint condition, with pride, joy, and hope.

CHOOSING A LIFE PARTNER

To acquire land, make haste.
To pick a mate, deliberate slowly.

Yevamot 63a

The idea that we should not jump into the selection of a life partner is not a new one, or even a very deep one. The fact is, however, that many people often do so anyway. Have you not heard of love at first sight? There is just enough truth in that notion—that there is sufficient electricity and connection between people who find each other attractive—to overcome whatever ancient wisdom has been transmitted by our ancestors, the books we have read, and the teachings of many generations.

So how can we educate young people—and older people—about the importance of being cautious, deliberate, and prudent when making this decision? How can we advise people whose hormones are raging, passionate lovers who tend to think only of the moment and do not project very far into the future, to take enough time to make a careful and reasoned choice in picking a life partner? The Rabbis in the statement make a comparison, one that I think works very well. In a less elegant way, I would advise that buying real estate and choosing a spouse are not done with the same haste; it is far easier to get out of the first decision, if it proves unworkable, than the second. If you purchase something and it does not fit, you take it back, or you sell it on eBay. With a large investment of funds, it's not quite as easy as running back to Macy's and getting a refund, but there is still no wrenching emotional crisis, as there is in divorce. For that matter, even if two people decide to live together without being married and then choose to sever the relationship, it is far more difficult than selling a house.

So the Rabbis put all of this in perspective by comparing choosing a mate to a far less loaded decision. The point they want to convey is that one of these decisions can be made rapidly, with perhaps only minor long-term consequences, usually financial, if it turns out to be a mistake. The other decision can have serious long-term effects on the wallet, too, but more important are its effects on the heart and soul, and in most cases, on the rest of your life. Another way of looking at it is that a property can be grabbed up by someone else in an hour—or less—if you wait; hesitation can be dangerous when buying property. By contrast, hesitation and careful thought are necessary prerequisites when choosing a mate. Whereas haste can be useful in the field of business, it is often disastrous in the realm of human relationships.

It's fairly amazing that the sages were able to convey such a profound lesson in so few words. This is the power of an aphorism. The Rabbis were master teachers, and the more we read their teachings, their values, and their ideas, the more respect and awe they generate in us.

COMPANIONSHIP

**Any man without a wife
endures life without joy,
without blessing,
without enjoyment.**

Yevamot 62b

I thought long and hard about including this statement. It may, in a way, come across as harsh and even insensitive. Not everyone is or has the opportunity to be married, including many people who want to be. So, is it cruel to say that someone who is not married is doomed to a life without joy and blessing? Without getting overly defensive about the rabbinic mind, it is well known that the ancient Rabbis had a penchant for exaggeration. But if this idea were framed in the positive instead of the negative, most of us would agree that there are benefits to love, companionship, and marriage.

I choose to understand this pronouncement as a position of advocacy for love and intimacy. Yes, a loving relationship brings joy, blessing, and contentment. And the absence of a warm, caring partner in life can leave a person without a sense of security, without someone to share the pleasures of life, and without someone on whose shoulder to cry when things are not going so well.

To live without a partner is not easy. As one who was divorced and lived for about a decade without a committed relationship, I can testify to the loneliness that attends such a lifestyle. Not everyone feels that way, but I did. Naturally there are substitutes for one permanent mate, but for me it was not the same. I experienced periods of loneliness, sadness, feeling lost, and even, at times, depression.

There were surely benefits. I could come and go as I pleased. I didn't have to check with anyone when making decisions—about how to spend my money, about where and when to travel, about whom to spend my time with, and dozens of other daily choices. But when evening came and I was alone, life did often seem to be without joy and satisfaction.

So I am all for intimacy, relationships, and marriage and partnership. The Rabbis could have probably expressed this view in softer words, but their point is clear. Life is meant to be spent with someone with whom you share interests, ideas, values, hopes, and dreams. Finding someone with whom you can have fun, build a history together, and learn how to live with is no easy task.

I think of the couples with whom I have celebrated long anniversaries—ten years, thirty years, fifty years. There is something very special about such long-term relationships. Growing older, and growing old together, can be a joy and a privilege. There's someone to lean on, someone to remember with, someone with whom you can look back at the years of life. And someone to dream with.

There are, as the Rabbis declare, blessings, joys, and satisfactions that come with caring, sharing, and intimacy.

THE GENERATION GAP

**Fortunate is the generation
in which the elders listen to the youth.**

Rosh Hashanah 25b

W hat makes some older people psychologically accessible to the
younger generation, and vice versa? In the sixties, conventional
wisdom told us that anyone under thirty could not trust anyone
over thirty. Forty years later, I'm not sure if things have changed
much.

Margaret Mead once observed that the only true natives in the
world are our youth. All the rest of us are visitors, foreigners. We
don't truly belong in the way that the vigorous, dynamic, youthful generation does, since it is they who are building our future.
They learn the language of the present as their mother tongue.
The technology, ideas, and cultural milieu of today's world is
understood by young people because they are creating it, fashion-
ing it in the direction in which they want it to go.

So what role do older people have in the process of societal
development? Is it not true that those over thirty established the
basis on which the new generation creates its norms? Isn't it the
older generation that built the platform of yesterday on which
stands the structure of today? Yes, but the cutting edge, the fresh

ideas, and the seedlings of tomorrow's world are being planted by those who are growing up right now.

Am I exaggerating the role of the young and underestimating the contribution of their parents and grandparents? Maybe. Or perhaps I am simply painting reality as it is, which is hard for those of us who have already lived most of our lives to accept. Do I still feel the juices of creativity bubbling inside my veins? Of course I do, and if I have something yet to contribute to the world, which I hope I do, it will be built upon the things I have already done—especially what I accomplished as a young person. I may be at the prime of my ability in certain ways, but if some day my life's contribution is measured, what I have achieved in my first fifty years will be the bulk of that contribution.

Think about it: it is the young poets, novelists, painters, scientists, economists, and medical researchers, who garner the lion's share of Nobel Prizes, even if their work is not recognized until many years later. Recipients of the award who are in their fifties, sixties, and seventies, are most likely being honored for discoveries and creations they achieved in their thirties or forties. Albert Einstein's theory of relativity came to him at a very young age, and he spent the remainder of his life refining it and searching for the next level to which to bring it. The Romantic poets John Keats and William Wordsworth and the naturalist essayists Henry David Thoreau and Ralph Waldo Emerson wrote most of their important works in the early part of their lives. In fact, most of these people did not live past forty or fifty. The same is true of the great classical musical composers, including Mozart, Felix Mendelssohn, and Franz Schubert.

So, the Talmud says, the "fortunate" generation is the one that pays serious attention to youthful contributions and creativity. But does not Jewish tradition tell us, in the biblical Book of Malachi, that the Messiah will come when the hearts of the children will turn to the hearts of their parents, and the hearts of the parents will turn to the hearts of the children? Meaning, there must be two-way communication between the generations. Why does the Talmud not say that the fortunate generation is the one in which the youth listen to their elders and the elders listen to the youth? Why is the expression in only one direction?

We cannot read the minds of the rabbinic masters, but we can make some educated guesses. Perhaps it is assumed that youth must listen to the older generation, and that often they do. They read the books, listen to the lectures, and watch the television documentaries of those who came before them. But the reverse is not true. Older people do not usually read the books of the younger generation, enjoy their music, dance their dances, or plumb their ideas and ideals. Perhaps that is why the Rabbis saw a fortunate generation as one in which the contributions of young people are taken seriously.

We can read into this rabbinic text what we want, and it may or may not have been intended by the author. But perhaps it is simply that the old in body should pay attention to the music, poetry, ideals, and innovative thrusts of the young in spirit, to that which is new and different and untried. And that the young part of our culture needs sufficient time and *attention* if it is to ripen and reach maturity. If that is what is meant, then who can argue with it?

UNCONDITIONAL LOVE

**All love that is dependent on a motive,
when the motive is gone, the love is gone.
Love that is not dependent on a motive
will endure forever.**

Avot 5:19

Humanistic psychologists of the twentieth century coined the phrase "unconditional love," but the sages of the Mishnah offered its perfect definition some two thousand years ago. This Talmudic statement could be translated as: love that is conditional can fail, but love that is unconditional will never fail. The upshot is that true, deep, and abiding love does not have conditions.

A parent who loves a child should not say (or feel), "If you get high grades in school, I will love you." That is conditional love. If the condition disappears, that is, if the child does poorly in school, should the parent lose his love for the child? A wife who loves her husband should not say (or feel), "If you earn a high salary, I will love you." That is conditional love. If the husband loses his job, or is forced to take a pay cut, should the wife lose her love for him? A person should not say (or feel) to a friend, "If you buy me expensive birthday gifts, I will love you." If the friend, for whatever (financial or other) reasons, stops lavishing the other with costly presents, should the person lose his love for his friend? That is conditional love.

People often dissolve marriages, break up friendships, and become estranged from family members for reasons that are hard to explain. The sense of commitment is weak in today's relationships. The Rabbis were trying to argue, I believe, for stronger relationships, ones that cannot be shaken by the winds of temporary events or volatile emotions.

Is it possible to unconditionally love someone who has harmed you, or committed a crime, or done evil to another person? I believe that if the love is sincere, deep, and authentic, it can last through many low points. There is a popular phrase that says we should hate a person's deeds, when they are inappropriate, but not the person. This makes sense.

Using the Talmudic standard for relationships and seeing love as a deep commitment that must withstand the storms of life will raise the level of society's moral fiber and strengthen the bonds of family and community.

V

Teaching and Learning: Methods, Goals, and Results

"The study of the Torah is more important than the rebuilding of the Temple in Jerusalem."

Megillah 16b

KNOWLEDGE GAINED
AND LOST

**Words of Torah are difficult to acquire,
precious like vessels of gold and rare metal;
but like fragile glass, easily broken and lost.**

Hagigah 15a

The acquisition of wisdom is a subject that strongly consumed the minds of the ancient sages. It was their métier, their major art form, and their most important preoccupation. Unlike the biblical prophets, who received their wisdom directly from God, it was the Rabbis' task to study, explain, and interpret the word of God and pass it on to the next generation. Their most precious resource was not expensive oils, sweet-smelling fragrances, rare wine, or valuable jewels, but the divinely created and matchless human mind. They spent days and nights pouring over the Torah, mining it for its prized gems. In Pirke Avot they said, "Turn it and turn it, for everything is in it." The Torah contains such important information and advice that we must search constantly for new and deeper meanings and interpretations. Or, as Midrash Rabbah frames it, the Torah has seventy faces.

Given this mind-set, how weighty it must have been for the Rabbis to discern the most effective methods of committing it to memory, and gaining permanent possession of its sacred words. We can conclude from this statement in Hagigah 15a that it was no easy task. Certain scholars were especially gifted in their capacity to memorize, but that was not their ultimate goal. Truly owning a block of information implied knowing not just the words, but also the ideas behind the words, the concepts and ideals that were the foundation of the words, and how it all fit together into the grand matrix of the Jewish way of life. Accomplishing this grand feat meant delving into the holy books chapter by chapter, verse by verse, word by word.

Talented pedagogues that they were, when the Rabbis presented an idea, they also laid bare its foil, the underbelly of the concept, its inherent limitations. It is an enormous challenge to become a person of wisdom and knowledge. Doing so meant giving up many precious hours that most people would prefer to spend on leisure activity. In the ancient Greco-Roman world in which the Rabbis lived and moved, they saw all around them individuals for whom the baths, the games, or perhaps more abstract and ethereal intellectual pursuits, such as mathematics or philosophy, were their passion. But for the Rabbis, focus was on discovering the finer points of the good life, on discovering God's will for the Master's creatures. They wanted to tease out the most important truths of the Torah so that their lives would be filled with a maximum degree of holiness.

This pursuit required untold hours of reading, discussion, debate, and imaginative embellishment, but it was surely worth its price in the Rabbis' value system. The flip side of the endeavor was that knowledge is like sand in your palm. It can easily fall through the cracks, slip down between the fingers, and blow away with the wind. The precious wisdom acquired through hard labor, and often strained argumentation, could just as easily be gone, lost, and undone. All the more reason to find ways to retain it, store it, protect it, and keep it from slipping away, as if a thief had come and stolen these most valuable possessions.

Being wise mortals, but mortals just the same, the Rabbis were all too aware of the mind's ability to forget, even that which was acquired by rigorous effort. It took repetition, relentless plodding, and reviewing the same material over and over again to transmute knowledge that at once resembled impenetrable gold and breakable fragile glass.

Anything rich in value is worth working hard for, and if it is Torah, the ultimate good and guide, it is worth spending your life on. At the same time we must be starkly aware that this precious commodity is easily lost. This dual nature of Torah knowledge was both its strength and its limitation. The Rabbis were not about to devote most of their waking hours on something that could disappear in the blink of an eye without putting up a good fight. And so they put into place all kinds of mechanisms to ensure that their prized possession—knowledge and understanding of the paths to holy living—would keep its lasting nature for as long as possible. Mostly it came down to repetition, persistence, focus, and prioritizing—and the awareness of both the strength and weakness of this invaluable product, which they have succeeded in keeping alive, dynamic, and central in the scheme of Jewish religion and tradition.

Learning by Teaching

Much have I learned from my teachers;
even more from my friends;
most of all from my students.

Taanit 7a

This Talmudic statement is, in a way, a continuation of the previous one from Hagigah 15a. It deals with the process of learning, the most effective techniques and practices that lead to good, solid, and deep learning.

Three levels of learning are described, in ascending order of effectiveness. We all learn a great deal, of course, from inspiring teachers. They are our role models, our mentors, and our masters. Think about the people who left the deepest impression on your soul, who imprinted a lasting mark on your personality. It might have been an early teacher in school or a relative or friend from childhood days. Our parents are, in most cases, our most influential teachers, even though they usually don't teach in the formal way a classroom teacher does, and not the same subject matter.

What our parents, relatives, neighbors, and other adults teach us is ultimately more important than what we gain in the formal setting of a school. They teach us how to be a person. How to be grateful, how to be optimistic, how to accept criticism, how to laugh at ourselves, and how to restrain our anger. These are lessons that are not found in books, not in kids' books anyway. We learn these things by watching and modeling. No one gets through life without using, or misusing, these important skills.

The second level of learning is what we get from our friends and peers. The tried-and-true method of study in the traditional yeshivah is learning with a *hevruta*, or learning partner. Far superior to learning on our own is sharing the experience with a companion. Several important things happen when we study with someone else. First of all, we usually say the words aloud, so both partners can hear them. Hearing the words reinforces the learning. Second, learning partners have an opportunity to clarify things that they may not comprehend. Each of the two people knows things the other does not, and by exchanging information, both gain. Third, a partner does not let the other person off the hook, as we might by ourselves. If we don't understand something, we can easily skip over it or rationalize to ourselves that we understand it well enough. With a partner, that will not work. A good learning partner will push until the issues are clear, the material is understood, and the questions are all answered as best as the two people can do.

The third and highest level of learning is when a person has to prepare a lesson and teach it to a group or class. If one partner will challenge us, a room full of learners will not let us sign off until the issue is chewed up and digested, until it is made as clear as earthly possible.

When we sit down with a text and know that we are responsible to help others comprehend it, we accept a much deeper responsibility than just the desire to gain information and knowledge. We will succeed only to the extent that we can convey the material in the clearest and fullest manner.

To teach a text we may have to do extensive background research, look up references, check word definitions, challenge all assumptions, and anticipate the angles and meanings we may be called upon to explain and elucidate. Teaching a text is a far different thing than learning a text, and the Rabbis understood that through their own personal experience.

The three levels enumerated in this statement are somewhat obvious, yet putting them in this order is useful in itself. There is also the surprise element in this statement. The Rabbis' ladder of learning is counterintuitive because conventional wisdom would say that we learn the most from our teachers and parents, some from our peers, and the least from our students, who know little and don't have much knowledge or experience to share. But here the acknowledgments are turned around. To teach a text or a subject well, we have to know it better than just learning it on our own, and for ourselves. And our students are our best teachers because their creative questions and demanding challenges push us to a deeper level of thought and analysis than we might go to by ourselves or even with another person.

WHEREIN LIES SECURITY?

**Who are the guardians of a city?
The teachers of Bible and Mishnah.**

Yerushalmi Hagigah 2

The question posed by the Jerusalem Talmud is one that all nations, leaders, and concerned people have been struggling with for millennia. What provides the real security of a city, a state, or a nation? Is it military might or moral power?

The answer, of course, is both. But if forced to choose between these two, which stands above the other?

When we hear the word "guard," perhaps we visualize a person with a gun. That is, a military figure or force of some kind. Who can protect the homes, institutions, and citizens of a city? The answer, as logic dictates, is an army that braces itself at the border and prevents its enemies from penetrating the walls and attacking. In this thinking, physical force stands up against physical force.

The Rabbis, however, are suggesting a more subtle and deep defense to prevent destruction of a city. The usual assumption is that destruction, if it comes, will come by foreign military attack. But there are other, less blatant ways that a city can fall apart. We are reminded of Edward Gibbon's *The Rise and Fall of the*

Roman Empire in which Gibbon argues that Rome fell not because of outside attackers but because of corruption within. The pedagogical directive of the Jerusalem Talmud takes a similar approach. It too posits that the worst and most common kind of failure of a community comes from within.

This kind of deterioration is one of inward moral rot. In other words, the worst and most effective enemy is the one we bring upon ourselves. It is the enemy of lapsed education, excessive materialism, narcissism, and ignoring the teachings of those who came before us.

By this reasoning, the best way to protect a city is by making its citizens strong in spirit. The question then becomes, "What makes a city strong enough to protect itself from destruction?" The Talmud's answer is that promotion of values and education provides strength. Certainly it is the values in the sacred texts that have kept the Jewish people strong through the centuries, along with following the rituals and adhering to the ethics handed down by our ancestors. Self-respect, fair ways of running a society, endorsing the values of truth, justice, compassion, and sensitivity—these are the most powerful weapons any society can store in its arsenal of self-defense. They are stronger than guns, tanks, and bombs.

The power of a society lies in the individuals and their principles, their spiritual fortitude, and their moral behavior. No weapon can destroy these sterling qualities. All of this explains why the teachers of Torah and Talmud are the most effective and important defenders of a city.

OUR CHILDREN, OUR FUTURE

**The world exists only because of
the breath of young students at school.**

Shabbat 119b

"That's what it's all about!" my synagogue's president declared after a delightful performance of the kindergarten class of our congregation.

I would venture to guess that every synagogue president, along with every parent and every Jew, believes that we devote our labors, our resources, and our time to ensure that the next generation will carry the values, commitments, and way of life that we have spent our lives promoting and protecting.

We take great pride in the institutions in our community that educate and acculturate our young—the next generation. We view our children as the bearers of our legacy. Just as we received a heritage from our parents, grandparents, and ancestors, so, too, do we hope that our children, grandchildren, and descendants for many generations will carry forward what we have received.

In Hebrew we have many words for our heritage—*yerushah, masoret, kabbalah*. They all point to the same thing: the wisdom, insights, values, and traditions that constitute the warp and woof of the Jewish way of life.

The greatest *nachas* (Yiddish for spiritual joy) any Jew can receive is to watch our young people demonstrate their commitment to our values. It may be a nursery school or kindergarten performance, a bar/bat mitzvah ceremony, a graduation, or some other joyous shared event that is a snapshot of what we try to teach on a daily basis in our schools. Children standing on the stage singing, chanting, or reciting words—sometimes in Hebrew—that describe what they have learned and proclaim how much they care about their parents' and teachers' wisdom is a tangible symbol of the entire educational process.

Many cultures share the passion for learning and passing on the literary legacy of past generations to the next one. The Jewish tradition is particularly strong in this respect.

In the Middle Ages, when other groups were protecting the knowledge of their sacred writings from the masses and it was only the political and religious leaders of the community who were allowed to learn how to read, Jewish communities were building schools and training teachers to ensure the widest possible dissemination of knowledge. The democratic thrust in Jewish education is one that began with the founding of Judaism itself. In the Torah (Deuteronomy 6:7) we are taught in one of the most important passages of scripture to "teach [these words] diligently to your children."

We can also examine the literary merits of this statement. The Rabbis could have simply stated that Jewish education is important. But as we know from the Torah, the biblical prophets, and all powerful and eloquent statespersons who have influenced the masses throughout the ages, language is a critical tool in the battle of persuasion. Martin Luther King, Jr., Winston Churchill, Abba Eban, and Rabbi Abraham Joshua Heschel were all international leaders whose ability to inspire was based in great part on their eloquent, elegant, and powerful formulation of ideas.

The ancient Rabbis use a phrase that is as unusual as it is graphic: "The breath of young students at school." One sees in the mind's eye a picture of young boys and girls sitting at their desks, speaking, reading, talking, struggling with texts and ideas. Their breath is a concrete symbol of their ability to formulate sounds, words, ideas, and value positions. What a remarkable metaphor, "the breath of school children." We don't picture stick figures parked at a desk. Rather, we see dynamic children thinking, moving, arguing, answering questions, and jumping in their seats with hands throbbing toward the teacher in order to be recognized. Breath equals life, dynamic and creative life. Only through such dynamic breath formulating and absorbing a thriving culture does any community have the potential to survive.

THE DANGERS OF IGNORANCE

**When an ignorant man is outwardly pious,
stay far away from him!**

Shabbat 63a

The apparent polarity between ritual and ethics, formal observance and moral behavior, is one that has been discussed and
debated from time immemorial.

The ancient Rabbis weigh in on this subject in our statement
above. The conflict here is not the conventional one—between
following halakhah (Jewish law) on the one hand and leading an
ethical life on the other. This conflict instead is between ritual
and knowledge. But in many ways the battle is the same. The
bottom-line questions are these: Can following rituals and customs stand alone? Can being a ritually observant Jew constitute
the totality of one's Jewishness, absent an understanding of the
meaning behind the rituals?

In the usual conflict, between ritual and ethics, what is
emphasized by theologians is that ritual must lead to proper
behavior. In the conflict described in this Talmudic statement, the clash is between engaging in formal, required
behaviors and having no intellectual understanding to under-
gird them.

In both cases, the point in some respects is the same: ritual alone—observance by itself—is not sufficient.

Some view focusing primarily on ritual as "mechanical," others think of it as empty actions, and still others regard such observance as half-baked religion. Rabbi Abraham Joshua Heschel called it "religious behaviorism." Few people see the thoughtless, perfunctory, unthinking performance of rituals as something positive.

Why not?

As far back as the eighth century the prophet Isaiah railed against those who brought sacrifices to the Temple and thought that this kind of obedience to the strict dictates of the law was meritorious. "*Kav le-kav, tzav le-tzav,*" said Isaiah, meaning that the recitation of formulaic mantras in place of heartfelt prayer was meaningless. In his first great oration, a powerful discourse on the sins of the nation, Isaiah complained of the people's childish approach to godly behavior in thinking that the mere act of bringing an animal to the altar would expunge their sins from the divine ledger. "'What need have I of all your sacrifices?' says God. 'I am sated with burnt offerings of rams and blood of bulls; I have no delight in lambs and he-goats. Who asked that of you—to trample my courts?'" (Isaiah 1:11–12).

In the same way, God cannot tolerate the performance of mitzvot and outward actions of piety that are bereft of a deep understanding of their purpose. The mitzvot were given, says the Talmud, "to purify human conduct." The outward forms of religion are designed to be symbols and reminders, to provide aesthetic patterns that constitute vessels of meaning, information, and inspiration.

Teachers and students are commanded to probe the background, history, and purpose of the mitzvot in order to grasp their moral and aesthetic design. Look not to the wrapping ("box," "can"), says Pirke Avot, but to what is inside. "Humans look to the appearance, while God explores the heart" (I Samuel 16:7).

The Rabbis thought of a scholar who did not practice the mitzvot as a donkey with a pile of books on its back. The opposite was also odious to them: a donkey who follows the paths of his master's whip but does not even have any books to carry.

The Rabbis in tractate Shabbat sought a religion that was authentic, serious, and firm, not one that was phony, outward, and flimsy. They wanted their adherents to uphold a way of life that had deep meaning and profound intellectual moorings, not an automatic set of actions that was an easy golden path to heaven in the minds of its practitioners.

Judaism has always been strongly based on books and ideas, so that outward behavior that was acceptable for a machine would not suffice for a thinking, sentient being created in the image of God. Thus, the seeming harshness of this Talmudic warning. Keep far from people who seek the easy path, those who mimic their neighbors in ritual acts that are devoid of moral and spiritual content. Judaism is a religion of high thinking and high acting, not a code for a cadre of blind-acting automatons. Think high. Surround yourself with high-thinking people. Then, and only then, will Judaism, its rituals, customs, and observances, bring joy, fulfillment, and meaning to life.

A LITTLE LEARNING IS A DANGEROUS THING

**A single coin in an empty vessel
makes a loud useless noise.**

Bava Metzia 85b

The lessons taught by the Rabbis regarding knowledge, education, and learning are abundant. Since education was the cornerstone of their life—the source of their values, the goal of their child-rearing, the preoccupation of the community, and the basis of the continuity of their tradition—we will find, combing through rabbinic literature, some statement about every aspect of the learning process and the results of education (or the lack thereof).

The Rabbis had ideas about how to learn, how to teach, how to motivate students, and the results of intensive education, as well as admonitions regarding when, how often, and why it is necessary to devote most of our leisure time to the pursuit of knowledge. Their writings are filled with comments and attitudes about people who study, those who ignore books, the importance of the hierarchy of scholars over nonscholars, the product of the right kind of education, and every other matter relating to study, learning, and teaching.

The admonition at hand relates to the level of knowledge of any given individual. We have spoken before of the rich use of metaphoric language in rabbinic teaching. They could have stated it this way: A person who knows very little makes noise in inverse proportion to his knowledge. But how mundane and lacking in literary grace would such a teaching be! The image of a single coin in a jar is one we are all familiar with. We can easily and clearly conjure, in our minds and ears, the irritating rattle and prattle of a single, useless, noisy coin rolling around, crackling against the edge of the vessel.

I think the Rabbis are implying two separate messages in this statement. First, to quote Alexander Pope (1688–1744; "An Essay on Criticism"): "A little learning is a dangerous thing; drink deep, or taste not the Pierian spring: there shallow draughts intoxicate the brain, and drinking largely sobers us again." This means something like, a small amount of knowledge can cause people to think they are more expert than they are and consequently to make unwise choices. Thinking we are more informed than is based in reality can bring all kinds of unfortunate consequences. Living in an illusion is rarely a healthy condition. In this case it can lead to boasting, arrogance, authoritarianism, and a multitude of other moral and psychological failures and sins.

But then the Rabbis hint at a further problem. That is, ignorance breeds a nest of complainers. More often than not, those who know the least make the most noise. They boost their sagging egos by shouting their ignorance loud enough to overcome the shrinking size of their information. So often the gripes and growls of the masses really stem from those who think they are experts but are not. There is a gaping inadequacy in the soul of a person who can never stand comfortably in a group of intelligent people who are at ease with themselves. Indeed that person's discomfort pushes him or her to hide it through diversionary tactics, such as turning up the volume of their sound. The equation works out to this: the less a person knows, the more he or she talks; the smaller his or her supply of information, the greater the frequency of his or her moaning and groaning.

Thus, we find once again that the ancient sages were wise in the ways of the human heart and soul, even without doctorates in clinical psychology—or even having heard of the term. Their life experience, their keen observation of human foibles, and their high-minded value system all combined to make them the grand teachers of their generation, and of generations to follow.

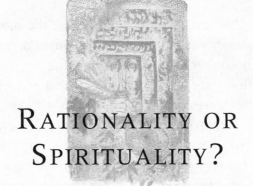

RATIONALITY OR SPIRITUALITY?

A sage ranks higher than a prophet.

Bava Batra 12a

The Rabbis of the Talmudic period established rankings in many areas. They loved to make comparisons. And often their comparisons would surprise a learner. As excellent pedagogues, they would sometimes use the element of surprise to announce the superiority of one type of person over another, especially when the expectation of students was that it might have been the other way around.

For example, in another such comparison, they declare that a child born of an illegal marriage who is learned is superior to a *kohen gadol* who is an ignoramus. I shake my head and smile when reading these kinds of comparisons. It's as if the Rabbis are saying, "You might think that the *kohen gadol*, the person who conducts the holiest ritual of the Jewish people, sacralizing the offerings of the masses, is the highest ranking individual in Jewish religious circles. Well, think again." It is not formal status that really counts, but the hard work of study and learning that, in the final analysis, gives a person importance and prestige.

It is the same in the quote here, though not quite as dramatic a comparison. Think about the status of these two individuals. The prophet receives a direct revelation from God. What could be more important than that? The great prophets of Israel are still the spiritual leaders of our people. Their soaring thoughts and majestic writings have left a legacy that impacts the moral and spiritual direction of many faiths and nations to this day. The prophetic pronouncements of the divinely inspired greats like Isaiah, Jeremiah, Amos, Hosea, and Micah continue to inspire.

And yet, anyone who delves into the holy books to become conversant with Jewish tradition, and who establishes himself or herself as an authority in areas of Jewish law and lore, surpasses the prophets in rank. A person need not be born into the holy priesthood, need not be a descendant of Aaron, brother of Moses, appointed by God to accept the sacrifices of the people at the holy altar. Instead, it is high intellectual ambition that marks the important person in Jewish life. Further, a person need not be designated as God's spokesperson, carrying the divine message to the masses, to be considered a person of exalted stature.

Knowledge is the key to Jewish life, especially during the rabbinic period and since then. Neither priest nor prophet equals the importance of the scholar, the teacher, or the wise sage who masters the vast body of biblical and rabbinic literature and can interpret, explain and transmit that heritage to the next generation. This way of thinking caused a sea change from the biblical to the rabbinic period. In the Tanakh it was the priest and prophet, *kohen* and *navi*, who were God's most important servants. But once the period of divine revelation was considered completed at the end of the biblical period, the ancient Rabbis declared the primacy of their role in Jewish life.

After the Temple had been destroyed in 70 CE, the role of the *kohen* was seriously diminished, if not for all practical purposes terminated. The role of the prophet was also lost, since the end of revelation caused the very act of prophecy, according to the Rabbis, to be turned over to children and fools. It was now in the hands of the scholars to carry forward the great heritage that had been received from God and passed on through God's emissaries, the biblical prophets.

No one could achieve a higher level of importance in Jewish society, from this point on, than the sage, the teacher.

This raises the question for us as to whether the fad in seeking "spirituality" is the most authentic and effective path to God. Spirituality is a buzzword that has caught the imagination of many people today, especially the young, who believe that ritual and formal religion is less important than what is found in the heart. In their view, each person is entitled to his or her own personalized religion.

If this implies that the moral, literary, and intellectual inheritance of the past three thousand years can be put aside in favor of "personal meaning" and noble, universal ideals, then rabbinic Judaism would have a strong quarrel with that position. *"Lo am ha-aretz hasid,"* say the Rabbis in Pirke Avot. An ignoramus cannot be pious (or spiritual, we might add). Knowledge is the base, the bottom line, the fundamental criterion for right behavior and proper understanding in Jewish thinking. It is not the mystic, the spiritualist, or the God-seeker, but the scholar, the teacher, and the average learned shopkeeper who takes pride of place in the hierarchy of Jewish life.

Of course, knowledge must lead to good deeds, in addition to a moral and spiritual life. But spirituality bereft of a rational basis will quickly evaporate. Thus, the Rabbis insisted that a knowledgeable Jew ranks higher than even the prophet of the Lord.

WISDOM IS INNATE

God only gives wisdom to one who already has wisdom.

Berakhot 55a

As noted in earlier chapters, one of the salient features of rabbinic teaching is that what is obvious on the surface is not necessarily so. The Rabbis play with our minds, not to tease or ridicule us, but to persuade us to pay attention. Today's conventional wisdom might say that only a person without wisdom needs God's wisdom. Not so, say the rabbinic teachers. It takes wisdom to gain wisdom seems to be their understanding. This is counterintuitive, but once we think about this idea more carefully and analytically, it makes sense.

On the most obvious level—and probably not the one the Rabbis intended—a person needs to have a modicum of intelligence and wisdom to absorb more wisdom. An empty-headed person would not know where to put the new information. It reminds me of when I clean the lint catcher in my dryer. When I can't make it stick to my fingers, I take some lint from one corner and use it to attract more lint. Like attracts like. So, too, wisdom attracts wisdom.

On a higher level, it seems to me that unless a person is wise to begin with, he or she will not see the need for more wisdom. A person who is wise, who understands the purpose and uses of wisdom, will grasp its importance and utilize it to its best advantage. Such a person will derive satisfaction from whatever wisdom he or she has, and will want more, search for more, and be open to receiving more. When God senses that, God will provide it.

There is an even higher level of meaning to this statement. Wisdom, I believe, is something divinely ordained. All people have it. The more wisdom we have, the more we want, the more we will be prone to use it in our daily comings and goings, our experiences and interchanges with others. When it becomes a routine part of our being, a regular experience from which we derive satisfaction and fulfillment, there is no reason why we would not crave more. But the initial seeds have to be there so that the plant of wisdom can grow and become beautiful to see and smell and provide pleasure to all who are near it.

There is more. Because wisdom is God-given, intuitive, and a part of all people, it is a commodity that reproduces itself. The qualities of wisdom are such that it will recognize like-minded information and experience. It will attach itself to similar wisdom.

When I was a young therapist-in-training, I was taught how to gather information so that I could understand a client's issues, fears, and life situation. In the course of training, one experienced therapist said to me, "We really cannot train a person who does not already have the inclination to be a therapist. A person who has the intuitive understanding of people, a sense of compassion for others, and a desire to be of help is 'trainable.' Someone without basic intuitive interpersonal skills cannot be trained to acquire them. You can hone the skills of a therapist, but you cannot make a therapist of someone who does not have the initial equipment."

I think it is the same with wisdom. If a person is wise, he or she can become even more wise. But without the seeds of wisdom that are ready to blossom if watered and given sunshine and ten-der loving care, it cannot grow bigger and greater. So, paradoxi-cally, we need wisdom to get wisdom. That's what the Rabbis are saying. God only gives wisdom to those who already have it.

VI

Life's Puzzles: A Potpourri of Solutions to Everyday Problems

"God created the evil inclination, but also the Torah as the antidote."

Bava Batra 16a

DEFINING MIRACLES

**Earning a living is similar in difficulty
to the parting of the Reed Sea.**

Pesachim 118a

Two possible interpretations of this statement come to mind. The first is that making enough money to sustain yourself (and other dependents) is no easy task. There are very few people for whom earning money comes easily. Whether you make a large salary or a small salary, whether the work is physical or intellectual, whether you love your work or hate it, it requires a large investment of time, persistence, and strength of body and/or mind to make an adequate living.

In typical rabbinic style, the hyperbolic nature of this maxim impresses upon the reader the idea that rare is the person for whom adequate funds come easily. "Splitting the Reed Sea" is a common Talmudic metaphor for something that is very difficult, something that only a miraculous intervention from the divine could accomplish. In other words, to make a decent living, you need divine intervention because the average person has so many obstacles to overcome, and so many (difficult) people to deal with. There are many things that can and do go wrong, and most of us have our ups and downs in assuring a steady income. I recall the oft-repeated saying I heard while serving in the U.S. Army as a military chaplain at the beginning of my career: "If something can go wrong, it will." This applies to much of life, and not just to the military. But in the military when something goes wrong, it can cost lives, so emphasis is on anticipating the worst possibilities at all times. Likewise, anticipation can lessen the potential obstacles that could arise in the workplace.

This seems like a valid interpretation of this quote on the surface. But if we delve more deeply, there may be another level of exegesis that teaches a more important lesson.

The first interpretation views the splitting of the Reed Sea as something too difficult for humans to accomplish without some divine assistance. But let's think of the parting of the waters of the Reed Sea as a paradigm of a miracle. In other words, let's consider not the difficulty of the task, but the theological implications. What does this teach us about the comparison between earning a living and the Israelites marching into the high waters to find dry land and then walking to safety while their Egyptian pursuers drown?

If we look at *k'riyat yam suf* (the parting of the Reed Sea) as a miracle rather than as something that is very difficult (assuming that miracles are not all that difficult for the Creator, who can make anything happen), we can then see that earning a living is a miracle in the same theological sense. How so?

If someone is a farmer, he or she has to rely on the "miracles" of the sun shining, the rain falling, the seeds growing, and so on. These daily miracles are a part of how we all sustain ourselves. In similar fashion, there are countless daily miracles associated with any occupation. For a doctor, the healing process is surely a miracle. For a tailor, cotton, linen, and wool are provided miraculously by the ongoing birth and growth of God's creatures.

This second interpretation means that the daily requirements of human sustenance are dependent on God's watchful participation in the creative process. It is no less a miracle that we produce food, clothing, and all the products and services that humans rely on than is the parting of the Reed Sea. There are as many miracles in earning a living as there are in the biblical acts of intervention that God caused millennia ago to bring salvation and redemption to the world.

Therefore, do not take for granted the simple things that come our way every day. Do not think of miracles only as a grand interruption of nature caused by God. Just as miraculous are the routine occurrences of daily life—awakening in the morning and seeing the sun, watching trees grow from the ground, or marveling at magnificent buildings that are made from the wood of trees and the bricks that have been baked in the sun. Our ability to make a living requires God's daily miracles—as the siddur says, "the miracles that are daily with us, evening, morning and noon."

Albert Einstein said it beautifully in these words: "There are only two ways to live your life. One is as though nothing is a miracle. The other is as though everything is a miracle."

EFFORT VERSUS REWARD

If someone tells you:
"I labored but didn't get results—"
don't believe him.
"I did not labor, but got results—"
don't believe him.
"I labored and got results—"
[only then] believe him.

Megillah 6b

I am often surprised by some Talmudic gems that I have never come across in all the years of my reading and studying. But this one I found as a rabbinical student, and I immediately fell in love with it. It is so direct and it makes a great deal of sense.

This saying reminds me of another one, which says, "All generalizations are false—including this one!" Why? Because it makes a lot of sense, but it does not cover every case. Does every person who labors get results? Surely not. Does someone who does little occasionally get results anyway? For sure. But do most people who work hard ultimately get some kind of positive result? I believe so.

Looking back over the many years that I have spent writing, I can say that, in general, the pieces I have done in haste and have not rewritten or checked came out mediocre. However, when I labored on a piece with blood, sweat, and tears, the results bore witness to that. When I reread, rewrote, corrected, changed things, and even started over, the end product made me proud.

When I was in elementary school, I saw a documentary movie called *Dr. Ehrlich's 606*. It made a lasting impression on me. Dr. Paul Ehrlich, a Nobel Prize winner from Germany, was the inventor of a successful treatment for a sexually transmitted disease in 1909. The film showed how Dr. Ehrlich experimented hundreds of times with different possible treatments. Finally, in his 606th attempt, he succeeded. Imagine the persistence of this scholarly researcher. It is truly amazing. I have no doubt that the same dogged perseverance is present in the work of other inventors and scientists.

Many musicians write and rewrite their compositions to get them just right. The conclusion of Beethoven's fifth symphony went through nine different drafts. The Midrash tells us that even God went on creating worlds and destroying them until coming up with this one and declaring "This one pleases Me; those did not please Me" (Bereshit Rabbah 3:7).

This splendid aphorism offers an attitude of optimism, encouragement, and positivity. It gives us courage and confidence that our work will bring good results if we try hard enough—that persistent labor brings satisfaction and achievement to those who have a clear goal and enough gumption and perseverance to see it through.

There may be one more thing that attracts the reader to this wise advice. There is a bit of clever and biting humor that pokes fun at those among us who boast too much. We hear from time to time that this one had a meteoric rise in his corporation without any real effort. Or that one discovered a method of losing weight that came to her in a dream. Such ridiculous claims are so much wind in the tunnel. The Rabbis warn us: don't believe them. The snake-oil salespeople of the world will eventually be caught. Fakery does not cut the mustard. It is hard work, and more hard work, that brings home the prize.

QUANTITY OR QUALITY?

**One may do more, another may do less,
both are acceptable,
as long as the heart is directed to heaven.**

Berakhot 17a

This is a priceless Talmudic saying that I would like to paint as a sign over the office of the Chief Rabbinate in Israel. Maybe I'm too harsh, or too angry, about the extremes to which some of my more traditional coreligionists are going these days. The winds of fanaticism have blown strong over *Haredi* (extreme traditionalist) Jews.

They have lost sight of the big picture. Every last speck of Jewish law is treated as though the whole halakhic system will collapse if it is violated. It has become a matter of black and white, with no shades of gray in between to bring a nuanced definition of observance. My favorite definition of a Jew, which I learned from Rabbi Louis Finkelstein, late chancellor of The Jewish Theological Seminary of America, is that a good Jew is someone who is always trying to be a better Jew. There is a ladder of Jewish observance and ritual that we climb throughout life. One step at a time. Not all or nothing. We cannot jump to the top step of a ladder. We must climb slowly, and it is okay if we don't make it all the way, as long as we make a sincere attempt to keep climbing as high and as best as we can.

This is the mature, realistic, and intelligent approach that the sages of the rabbinic period took. Today things are so different, which upsets me and, I believe, the majority of Jews.

The irony is that the extremism, which has clouded religion and politics in the past decade or so, is not really in the spirit of traditional Judaism. Those who try to prove that they are superior to their less observant coreligionists are defeating the purpose of the whole enterprise. If they would study statements like this one from Berakhot 17a, they would come down off their pedestals and live in the real world.

It is a travesty that a rich, solid, four-thousand-year-old tradition that has proved itself so reasonable and advanced is perverted by some of its staunch self-appointed defenders who misinterpret its teachings and lead their followers astray.

The real question, missed by so many extremists, is simply this: where is the heart?

The prevailing religion among too many today is that they must do every tiny little law and custom that is possible to perform; otherwise, they are sinning. That's not my Judaism, nor is it, I think, the Judaism of the classical period of Jewish religious history. That Judaism combined the best of traditional ritual with the authenticity, honesty, and genuineness of the human soul.

The teaching we discuss here is beautiful and supremely important, one that should be taught to every Jewish child growing up in the tradition. Of course, the children must also be taught what it does *not* mean. It does not mean that you can do as little as you wish, as long as you mean it. But it does mean, in my humble opinion, that God measures our goodness and realness in terms of quality, not quantity. Those who love tradition, ritual, and celebration must do so with all their heart and soul. And if it is not every single word in the *Shulkhan Arukh* (Code of Jewish Law), so be it.

There is a delightful saying that the Hasidim love God and the *Mitnagdim* (those opposed to Hasidism) love the *Shulkhan Arukh*. It is a biting remark, but we live in a time when reality has to be shaken into the heads of those who are spreading false messages to their followers.

Ritual counts for a lot. But heart counts for even more.

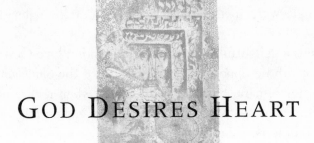

GOD DESIRES HEART

**The Blessed Holy One
desires heart!**

Sanhedrin 106b

In the aphorism discussed in the previous chapter, we examined an aspect of the metaphor of "heart" in religious practice. Now let's we look at a different idea that "heart" represents.

Human beings are wired differently. Some are more left-brain oriented, that is, rational and linear thinking. Some are more right-brain focused, that is, emotional and connected deeply to their feelings. Neither is better than the other. In fact, we are all both—in every human brain there resides the capacity for rational thinking and deep feeling. It is a matter of emphasis. In my experience, women are generally more feeling focused and men are more rationally oriented. I don't know if this is by nature or nurture. I suspect that at least part of it is ingrained in the sexes at birth, but it really does not affect this discussion.

One thing seems clear: many people are not in touch with their feelings and are not aware of what their emotions are at any given moment. Our society long believed that feelings were for the immature, and that an adult overcomes emotions simply by forming a stiff upper lip. The world watched in amazement and admiration when Jackie Kennedy displayed no tears at the funeral of her husband, President John F. Kennedy, on international television. Those of us with some psychological training felt differently, that this was not a healthy role model for the world. It would have been better had she evinced some emotional response to an event that upheaved her life, and the world. I related much more to the emotional display of Nancy Reagan at the funeral of her husband, President Ronald Reagan. Of course, it is not for me to judge the behavior of a new widow, and who knows how Jackie Kennedy grieved in private. Perhaps times changed between 1963 and 2004. In general, it seems more acceptable today to display emotions publicly, which is a healthy thing.

In the realm of religion, there is room for both clear thinking and deep emotion. Judaism prides itself on deep and constant learning. It takes a sharp mind and an avid and prodigious thinker, a rational person, to navigate and absorb the intricacies of Jewish law, of Talmudic reasoning, and of ethical decision making. There is also, however, a crucial role that emotion plays in the drama of religious celebration. The abundant rituals at festival celebrations, the profuse joy and emotion of life-cycle milestones, and the elation of community prayer that is such a vital part of the spiritual life of the Jew—all these provide space for the expressions of the heart.

What are some of the meanings of the Talmudic phrase, "The Blessed Holy One desires heart"?

We could start with: do not be among those who are heartless. Or: do not keep your emotions in tow. Give them free expression. In prayer, do not act like a robot, an automaton. Rabbi Abraham Joshua Heschel wrote often and eloquently about the sterile nature of American worship. The American synagogue, he wrote, is like a refrigerator. There is a great deal of decorum, but little warmth or emotion. We have responsive readings, said Rabbi Heschel, but he advocated a response from the heart. In

Heschel's book *God In Search of Man*, he writes of the pathos of God. In the Tanakh God expresses feelings, gets angry, feels pity, shows compassion. The biblical God is not the Aristotelian God—an unmoved Mover. God, according to Heschel, is the *most* moved Mover.

In Jewish prayer, ritual performance, and interpersonal relations, God wants heart. If there were more heart in the world, there would be less fighting, fewer wars, deeper spirituality, and closer friendships, marriages, and families.

Heart is the key to a complete, healed, and redeemed world. No wonder the Blessed Holy One desires heart.

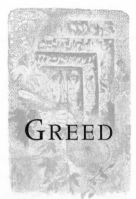

GREED

When you grasp too much you lose it all.
When you grasp a small portion, you win it all.

Hagigah 17a

This proverb is not one of the most profound philosophical revelations found in the Talmud, but it is a very helpful one for several reasons. First, it makes excellent sense. It is one of those truisms we all know, but when we hear it expressed succinctly, we immediately shake our heads as if to say, "Wow, that's so true!"

Second, it is easy to remember. In the Hebrew, the word *tafasta*—grab, or take, or reach for—is repeated four times in a sentence of only seven words.

Third, its obvious truth resonates with anyone who reads it. We have all had the experience, on occasion, of hoping to seize as much as we can, only to drop the whole thing because it was too heavy or too unwieldy and come away with nothing. It's like a waiter who tries to clear an entire table in one trip, and the whole tray falls on the floor and everything breaks into small pieces. Meanwhile the waiter at the next table, who made two or three trips, took a bit longer but didn't break a single dish or glass.

And fourth, because the common sense of this statement is so obvious, the occasion to quote it arises often. It captures a human

151

foible that is so pervasive and universal that perhaps we raise our-selves a notch higher in wisdom when we hear it and give heed to its message.

We can understand the statement literally—namely, grasping with the hands. On another level, a metaphoric one, there is grasping something intellectually. A student can sign up for too many courses in one semester. That, too, is grasping too much, increasing the probability of doing poorly in all the courses because of overreaching. A person can matriculate in law or med-ical school and drop out after the first year because the subject matter is above his or her mental ability. In Talmudic terminol-ogy a student can make a vow to study a full tractate each week—something only advanced and highly competent students can tackle—and then find that the demands of the commitment are simply too much.

There are so many examples that bear out the truth of this proverb because its wisdom applies to almost every area of life. The adage reflects a keen insight into human nature and provides a quick and simple solution to an all-too-human failure—biting off more than we can chew. All of us try to do too many things in too small a space of time. All of us, at one time or another, attempt to achieve things beyond our capacity.

Sometimes it is the simplest advice, which we too often ignore, that helps the most.

DOES A SIN CONTAMINATE
A SCHOLAR?

Even though a nut may have its shell soiled,
what's inside is still valuable;
in the same way, a scholar who has sinned
still holds valuable knowledge inside.

Hagigah 15b

Among the humane qualities that characterize the Talmudic sages we can count the following: realistic, compassionate, moderate, mature, wise, and inclusive. This is not to say that they had no standards, or that they were relativistic or permissive. At times some scholars demanded strict and high standards.

In general, however, the thrust of rabbinic morality and halakhah was reason, understanding, and acceptance. There is the famous dictum, "We may not impose on the community a decree that a majority of the people cannot live by" (Bava Batra 60b). This important reality check was part of the rabbinic criteria for legislating moral and ritual standards.

In the dictum we are examining here, the Rabbis deal with a situation they must have faced countless times, just as we, in modern days, often confront the same dilemma. How often do we hear about leading rabbinic figures who commit acts that are considered far beyond the pale of acceptable ethical standards? It is all too common to read about religious figures who act unethically and immorally in financial matters, in dealing with children, and in other interpersonal situations.

On the surface, this statement from Hagigah 15b does not extend an unreserved amnesty to such people. What I think the Rabbis are trying to say here is that we must not be overly pious when it comes to judging highly respected people. They should stand up to the same high standards that the rest of us are judged by, but they should not have to live up to impossibly high standards simply because of their exalted positions.

"Judge not another until you are in that person's position" (Pirke Avot 2:5) is good advice. Still, there are punishments, jails, and other remedies to keep society living up to accepted rules of decency and propriety.

What the Rabbis are saying, I believe, is that even the most distinguished scholars and leaders of the generation are prone to missteps from time to time, and this does not, need not, and should not totally tarnish their reputation in terms of the good things they have accomplished.

When the less-than-presidential behavior of Bill Clinton became public in 1998, many of his political opponents called for his impeachment and removal from office. It is my recollection, however, that while no one condoned the president's behavior, or even excused this failure in his personal life, very few people wanted him bounced from the Oval Office. At the time, many rabbis gave sermons in which they used King David as an example of someone who committed a terrible sin in the case of his relationship with Bathsheba. Together with condemnation of King David was the recognition that he was also the greatest Israelite king of all times, the Sweet Singer of Israel, the ancestor of the Messiah, and someone with a host of military, political, and literary accomplishments. When we think back in history, or peer into the siddur, the reputation of King David was surely sullied but by no means destroyed by this unforgivable behavior.

There are innumerable examples of the sages using clever metaphors to prove their points, and this statement is no exception. A nut that is filthy on the outside is not disqualified from tasting delicious. What a perfect way to convey the idea that while every person has some smudge attached to their garments, their overall character is not necessarily undermined, and their reputation as a moral individual is not necessarily completely ruined. We hope there is room for *teshuvah*, repentance, and that one, or even a few bad acts, don't strike out the reputation that a person has attained through goodness, scholarship, and other positive accomplishments.

JEWISH SOVEREIGNTY

**Whoever acquires a Hebrew servant
acquires a master.**

Kiddushin 20a

Some say that history has made Jews uncomfortable with power. In the modern State of Israel, power is a commodity that is taking a long time to handle adroitly and morally. Given the massive anti-Semitism that led to its creation and the anti-Zionism it has faced since day one, Israel—its leaders and governments—has done remarkably well in exercising its power for the first time in two thousand years. Despite the accusations of colonialism and occupation, among countless other unfair and unjust epithets hurled at the Jewish state, it has handled its newfound military power with an amazing degree of gentleness and compassion. Of course, not everyone would agree, and Israel's record in its five-plus decades of statehood is by no means perfect. But by the measure of nations in general, and given the political climate in Israel's regional neighborhood, I think Israel deserves high marks for how it has dealt with its military strength.

A glaring example of this point is the way Israel handled its incursion into the Palestinian stronghold of Jenin in spring 2004, when the military sacrificed dozens of Israeli soldiers in house-to-house combat instead of carpet bombing the town, which would have risked the deaths of many Palestinians. At the time, U.N. Secretary-General Kofi Annan said he was "frankly appalled" at Israel's behavior in Jenin, despite its having been very high by any moral standard.

This same moral consideration was demonstrated from the beginning of Israel's history, when the principle of *tohar ha-neshek*—purity of arms—was advocated. This meant that Israel's use of firepower was measured with careful preciseness so as to protect civilian lives and cause minimal collateral damage to noncombatants. During the Six Day War, when Israel liberated the Old City of Jerusalem with hand-to-hand and house-to-house combat, it absorbed higher losses of life than it would have had it bombarded the city with firepower; it also reduced the possibility of doing harm to Christian and Muslim holy sites.

So how does all of this tie in to our Talmudic statement above? In biblical times it was possible for a Jew/Hebrew to acquire another Hebrew as a servant. If a person indebted himself to the point of not being able to rise above the financial flood, one way out was to be a servant to the debtor for a period of time. But Jewish law protected the servant in so many ways that it made it difficult for the master to make full use of the servant; when one Hebrew acquired another as a servant, it was almost like getting a master rather than a servant. So protected were the rights of the servant that, in the view of the Talmud, it was almost not worth having one. There was the obligation to house, feed, and care for the servant, and to see to it that every amenity for servants was available. It was like having another child in the house. Thus, following the strictures of halakhah made it a burden rather than a benefit.

While at first blush the Talmud sounds like it is voicing a grievance, I read it as a commentary on the moral character of Jewish law. It manifests such a strong sense of fairness, kindness, and thoughtfulness—a standard of morality that is admirable. Pirke Avot says, *"S'na et ha-rabbanut,"* or "hate lordship." Jews have often been the victims of others' power and authority and therefore know all too well what the dangers of being the master, the boss, the king, the tyrant, or the czar are. And Jews have been trained—through centuries of experience and through a treasured legal system and social conditioning—that being in charge of the destiny of others is not easy or pleasant, and it is not necessarily even a good thing. Having control over others is a condition that invites inequity, so a tradition that espouses equality, fairness, and justice is simply not comfortable with it.

Admitting Ignorance

Teach your tongue to say:
"I don't know."
Lest you get caught lying.

Berakhot 4a

This aphorism takes the form of a warning, and a possible consequence. My preference is to emphasize the first half and not pay
too much attention to the second half. I am not concerned with
someone getting caught lying, because I think the act of admitting ignorance has a more important benefit than any potential
negative consequence of doing so.

Let's begin with what the Talmud seems to be saying. The pre-
sumption is that a person who is afraid to admit ignorance will
hide the fact that he or she does not know the answer, or the
information, and make something up to pretend expertise or
scholarship. It is probably true that in such situations, feigned
familiarity with a subject ends up making the speaker look like
both a liar and a fraud. It is surely more advisable to admit the
truth than to fudge the facts and pretend to know more than you
do. Lying ultimately compels a person to tell more lies to cover
up the first one, so that lying becomes a habit. And the reluc-
tance to tell the truth about not knowing fades with time.

What is behind the act of pretending to know something? It could be the desire to appear more informed, intelligent, and expert than a person really is. It might be the embarrassment of not knowing something a person thinks he should know. For example, a professor in a college classroom or an "expert" who is being interviewed on television might not want to admit a lack of information. After all, such a person is in a position in which knowledge is his trade. The public expects him to know everything there is to know in his field.

Thus, the advice is wise. Put aside pride and potential shame and admit the truth: you are not some superhuman creature who knows everything there is to know on a given subject. In this information age, in which specialists and sub-specialists abound, it is really impossible to have that much information committed to memory. A scholar or an expert is not someone who knows everything in her area of expertise. Rather she is a person who knows where to find the answer to any question in her field—if indeed an answer exists.

So saying "I don't know" is not such a terrible thing after all. It's the sign of a person who has enough self-esteem to realize that not knowing is not something to be ashamed of, but rather a part of being a wise person. Lying or hiding behind falsified information is necessary only for people with low self-esteem, people who need to cover up a phony, bloated image that they have created for public consumption.

As I mentioned earlier, my view is that the benefits of saying "I don't know" outweigh any possible negative consequences it may have. One such benefit is not coming off as a feigned braggart.

Anyone who has ever studied the writings and teachings of Rashi (Rabbi Shlomo Yitzhaki of Troyes; eleventh century) knows that this greatest of medieval Bible commentators frequently used the expressed, *"Aynee Yoday'a"*—I don't know. Rashi is a prime example of the kind of person who can admit to ignorance. It takes someone with a strong sense of self, and broad self-confidence, to state openly, and for posterity, "I don't know."

When someone has taught his tongue to say "I don't know," it is evident that there is so much that this person *does* know, and that not knowing every last fact or detail of a subject is nothing to be ashamed of. If an eleventh-century scholar can say "I don't know," then surely in the twenty-first century—when there is so much information available on everything—there is no need to be embarrassed about admitting to a lack of knowledge.

Thus, when I say that I prefer to emphasize the first half of this aphorism, I am less concerned with someone getting caught in telling tall tales—though I certainly don't admire that—than I am with a person's ability to admit the truth. And I would like to highlight the respect such an individual deserves from anyone listening. Rather than being a sign of weakness, it is a sign of great strength.

All hail to those who are confident and intelligent enough to admit "I don't know!"

BE A BELIEVER, BUT ALSO BE A HUMANIST

**One must be straight with other humans
the same way one is straight with the Omnipresent.**

Talmud Yerushalmi, Shekalim 3

In many ways, and in many traditional Jewish sources, the ancient Rabbis made valiant attempts to balance the need to be a good human being with the obligation to act as a loyal servant of God. As Rabbi Mordecai Kaplan told me, the job of Jewish tradition is to make its people into Jews and also to make its Jews into people. The late Virginia Satir, one of the world's master family therapists, titled her most popular book *Peoplemaking*. In all her work she tried to help people grow up into the people they were born to be. We are created in God's image and spend all our lives trying to live up to that high calling. It is surely a lifelong task, that is, making people into people—real, more complete, and more fulfilled.

To fully grasp the meaning of the important statement we are exploring now, we have to understand what prompted it. The Rabbis, of course, were pious scholars, deeply devoted to God and God's mitzvot. Living in what the Talmud refers to as "the four ells of the Halakah" (Berakhot 5a), meaning the restricted domain of Jewish law, by observing Jewish ritual, holidays, and life-cycle events, was a major priority for them. They spent their leisure time studying and doing good deeds, fulfilling God's law in minute detail.

But to the Talmudic Rabbis, ethics was just as important—in fact even more important—than ritual law. In one well-known and oft-quoted saying, "The mitzvot were given mainly to purify the heart of humans." When we talk about religion in the modern age, we immediately think of ritual observance—observing Shabbat, reciting the proper prayers at the proper time, wearing a tallit, keeping kosher, circumcising our boys on the eighth day after their birth, studying the Torah, and all the other countless ways we try to fulfill God's will. But many people, including me, make the distinction between being *observant* and being *religious*. The two overlap, but they are not identical.

God's law contains both what is called in the tradition *mitzvot she-bayn adam la-Makom*—mitzvot that govern the relationship between humans and their Maker—and *mitzvot she-bayn adam la-havero*—mitzvot that govern the relationships between people and their family, friends, neighbors, and others (that is, relationships between people and other people). It is possible to see this distinction in the two tablets of the Ten Commandments. The first tablet is made up of commands that relate to humans and God (the fifth, honoring parents, is the bridge command that falls into both categories), and the second tablet is focused on mitzvot between humans and other humans.

Striking this balance is a crucial aspect of being a Jew. You cannot be a good Jew unless you are also a good person (a *mensch*, in Yiddish). And as Jews, in the thinking of the rabbinic mind, you cannot be a good person in the fullest sense unless you fulfill the mitzvot that bind humans to God through ritual, prayer, study, and observance. The two go hand in hand. They feed and strengthen each other. The mitzvot are a system of "symbols," according to the late Professor Louis Finkelstein of The Jewish Theological Seminary of America, that help point a person's spiritual rudder toward being a God-like person.

The dichotomy between ritual and ethics is an old one, and everyone who deals with religion has had to face at one time or another the implications of going too far in either direction. The late scholar and teacher Maurice Samuel once said that trying to be a good person while ignoring the rituals and ceremonies that reinforce the ideals behind this goal is like a beautiful rose that has been plucked from its roots. It will retain its pleasing smell and colorful beauty for a few days, but then it will die. So, too, explained Samuel, a code of ethics that is detached from a system of beliefs and rituals will succeed for a generation perhaps; the real test is whether it will extend to the next generation without the scaffolding that supports the belief structure.

Rabbi Emanuel Rackman, former chancellor of Bar-Ilan University near Tel Aviv, and a distinguished scholar and Orthodox educator, describes an apartment building in Tel Aviv that permits only *shomray Shabbat* (strict Sabbath observers) to be accepted as residents. No cars are permitted to enter or leave the building on Shabbat, and you cannot live there without a commitment to follow all the strictures of Shabbat observance. But, adds Dr. Rackman—and here is the punch line—you can be a bank robber, a drug dealer, or even a murderer and be admitted into this specialized club of observant Jews. No one in the administrative office asks any questions of applicants that are related to matters that have to do with mitzvot between people and people; they ask only about issues that relate to humans and their obligations to God.

Thus, our Rabbis say a lot in a few words—that we cannot expect to be straight with God while ignoring our duties to live in the world with all the other creatures God put here, along with us.

SUGGESTIONS FOR
FURTHER READING

Adler, Morris. *The World of the Talmud*. New York: Schocken, 1963.

Bleefeld, Bardley, and Robert L. Shook, eds. *Saving the World Entire: And 100 Other Beloved Parables from the Talmud*. New York: Plume, 1998.

Bokser, Ben Zion. *The Talmud: Selected Writings*. New York: Paulist Press, 1989.

———. *The Wisdom of the Talmud: A Thousand Years of Jewish Thought*. New York: Philosophical Library, Inc., 1951.

Cohen, A. *Everyman's Talmud*. New York: E. P. Dutton 1949.

Corré, Alan. *Understanding the Talmud*. New York: KTAV, 1975.

Feinsilver, Alexander. *The Talmud for Today*. New York: St. Martin's Press, 1980.

Glatzer, Nahum N. ed. *In Time and Eternity: A Jewish Reader*. New York: Schocken Books, 1946.

Goldin, Judah. *The Living Talmud: The Wisdom of the Fathers and its Classical Commentaries*. New York: New American Library, 1957.

Hammer, Reuven. *The Classic Midrash: Tannaitic Commentaries on the Bible*. New York: Paulist Press, 1995.

Katz, Michael, and Gershon Schwartz. *Searching for Meaning in Midrash: Lessons for Everyday Living*. Philadelphia: Jewish Publication Society, 2002.

———. *Swimming in the Sea of the Talmud*. Philadelphia: Jewish Publication Society, 1998.

Kolatch, Alfred J. *Masters of the Talmud: Their Lives and Views*. Middle Village, NY: Jonathan David Publishers, 2003.

Lipman, Eugene J. *The Mishnah: Oral Teachings of Judaism*. New York: Norton, 1970.

Montefiore, C. G., and H. Loewe, eds. *A Rabbinic Anthology*. New York: Schocken Books, 1974.

Newman, Louis I., ed. *The Talmudic Anthology: Tales and Teachings of the Rabbis*. New York: Behrman House, Inc., 1945.

Petuchowski, Jakob J. *Our Masters Taught: Rabbinic Stories and Sayings*. New York: Crossroad, 1982.

Rubenstein, Jeffrey L. *Rabbinic Stories*. New York: Paulist Press, 2002.

Shapiro, Rami. *Ethics of the Sages: Pirke Avot—Annotated and Explained*. Woodstock, VT: SkyLight Paths Publishing, 2006.

———. *The Sacred Art of Lovingkindness: Preparing to Practice*. Woodstock, VT: SkyLight Paths Publishing, 2006.

Sherwin, Byron L., and Seymour J. Cohen. *Creating an Ethical Jewish Life: A Practical Introduction to Classic Teachings on How to Be a Jew*. Woodstock, VT: Jewish Lights Publising, 2001.

Siegel, Danny. *Where Heaven and Earth Touch: An Anthology of Midrash and Halachah*. Northvale, NJ: Jason Aronson, Inc., 1989.

Telushkin, Joseph. *The Book of Jewish Values: A Day-by-Day Guide to Ethical Living*. New York: Bell Tower, 2000.

Bar/Bat Mitzvah

The JGirl's Guide: The Young Jewish Woman's Handbook for Coming of Age
By Penina Adelman, Ali Feldman, and Shulamit Reinharz
An inspirational, interactive guidebook designed to help pre-teen Jewish girls address the spiritual, educational, and psychological issues surrounding coming of age in today's society.   6 x 9, 240 pp, Quality PB, 978-1-58023-215-9 **$14.99**
  Also Available: **The JGirl's Teacher's and Parent's Guide**
8½ x 11, 56 pp, PB, 978-1-58023-225-8 **$8.99**

Bar/Bat Mitzvah Basics: A Practical Family Guide to Coming of Age Together
Edited by Cantor Helen Leneman 6 x 9, 240 pp, Quality PB, 978-1-58023-151-0 **$18.95**

The Bar/Bat Mitzvah Memory Book, 2nd Edition: An Album for Treasuring the Spiritual Celebration By Rabbi Jeffrey K. Salkin and Nina Salkin
8 x 10, 48 pp, Deluxe HC, 2-color text, ribbon marker, 978-1-58023-263-0 **$19.99**

For Kids—Putting God on Your Guest List: How to Claim the Spiritual Meaning of Your Bar or Bat Mitzvah By Rabbi Jeffrey K. Salkin
6 x 9, 144 pp, Quality PB, 978-1-58023-015-5 **$14.99** *For ages 11–13*

Putting God on the Guest List, 3rd Edition: How to Reclaim the Spiritual Meaning of Your Child's Bar or Bat Mitzvah By Rabbi Jeffrey K. Salkin
6 x 9, 224 pp, Quality PB, 978-1-58023-222-7 **$16.99**; HC, 978-1-58023-260-9 **$24.99**
Also Available: **Putting God on the Guest List Teacher's Guide**
8½ x 11, 48 pp, PB, 978-1-58023-226-5 **$8.99**

Tough Questions Jews Ask: A Young Adult's Guide to Building a Jewish Life
By Rabbi Edward Feinstein 6 x 9, 160 pp, Quality PB, 978-1-58023-139-8 **$14.99** *For ages 12 & up*
Also Available: **Tough Questions Jews Ask Teacher's Guide**
8½ x 11, 72 pp, PB, 978-1-58023-187-9 **$8.95**

Bible Study/Midrash

Abraham's Bind & Other Bible Tales of Trickery, Folly, Mercy and Love *By Michael J. Caduto*
Re-imagines many biblical characters, retelling their stories and highlighting their foibles and strengths, their struggles and joys. Readers will learn that God has a way of working for them and through them, even today.
6 x 9, 224 pp, HC, 978-1-59473-186-0 **$19.99** *(A SkyLight Paths book)*

Ancient Secrets: Using the Stories of the Bible to Improve Our Everyday Lives
By Rabbi Levi Meier, PhD 5½ x 8½, 288 pp, Quality PB, 978-1-58023-064-3 **$16.95**

The Genesis of Leadership: What the Bible Teaches Us about Vision,
Values and Leading Change *By Rabbi Nathan Laufer; Foreword by Senator Joseph I. Lieberman*
Unlike other books on leadership, this one is rooted in the stories of the Bible, and teaches the values that the Bible believes are prerequisites for true leadership.
6 x 9, 288 pp, HC, 978-1-58023-241-8 **$24.99**

Hineini in Our Lives: Learning How to Respond to Others through 14 Biblical Texts and Personal Stories *By Norman J. Cohen* 6 x 9, 240 pp, Quality FB, 978-1-58023-274-6 **$16.99**

Moses and the Journey to Leadership: Timeless Lessons of Effective Management from the Bible and Today's Leaders *By Dr. Norman J. Cohen* 6 x 9, 250 pp, HC, 978-1-58023-227-2 **$21.99**

Self, Struggle & Change: Family Conflict Stories in Genesis and Their Healing Insights for Our Lives *By Norman J. Cohen* 6 x 9, 224 pp, Quality PB, 978-1-879045-66-8 **$18.99**

The Triumph of Eve & Other Subversive Bible Tales *By Matt Biers-Ariel*
5½ x 8½, 192 pp, Quality PB, 978-1-59473-176-1 **$14.99**; HC, 978-1-59473-040-5 **$19.99**
(A SkyLight Paths book)

Voices from Genesis: Guiding Us through the Stages of Life *By Norman J. Cohen*
6 x 9, 192 pp, Quality PB, 978-1-58023-118-3 **$16.95**

Or phone, fax, mail or e-mail to: **JEWISH LIGHTS Publishing**
Sunset Farm Offices, Route 4 • P.O. Box 237 • Woodstock, Vermont 05091
Tel: (802) 457-4000 • Fax: (802) 457-4004 • www.jewishlights.com
Credit card orders: (800) 962-4544 (8:30AM–5:30PM ET Monday–Friday)
Generous discounts on quantity orders. SATISFACTION GUARANTEED. Prices subject to change.

Congregation Resources

The Art of Public Prayer, 2nd Edition: Not for Clergy Only By Lawrence A. Hoffman
6 x 9, 272 pp, Quality PB, 978-1-893361-06-5 **$19.99** (A SkyLight Paths book)

Becoming a Congregation of Learners: Learning as a Key to Revitalizing
Congregational Life By Isa Aron, PhD; Foreword by Rabbi Lawrence A. Hoffman
6 x 9, 304 pp, Quality PB, 978-1-58023-089-6 **$19.95**

Finding a Spiritual Home: How a New Generation of Jews Can Transform the
American Synagogue By Rabbi Sidney Schwarz
6 x 9, 352 pp, Quality PB, 978-1-58023-185-5 **$19.95**

Jewish Pastoral Care, 2nd Edition: A Practical Handbook from Traditional &
Contemporary Sources Edited by Rabbi Dayle A. Friedman
6 x 9, 528 pp, HC, 978-1-58023-221-0 **$40.00**

Jewish Spiritual Direction: An Innovative Guide from Traditional and Contemporary
Sources Edited by Rabbi Howard A. Addison and Barbara Eve Breitman
6 x 9, 368 pp, HC, 978-1-58023-230-2 **$30.00**

The Self-Renewing Congregation: Organizational Strategies for Revitalizing
Congregational Life By Isa Aron, PhD; Foreword by Dr. Ron Wolfson
6 x 9, 304 pp, Quality PB, 978-1-58023-166-4 **$19.95**

Spiritual Community: The Power to Restore Hope, Commitment and Joy
By Rabbi David A. Teutsch, PhD 5½ x 8½, 144 pp, HC, 978-1-58023-270-8 **$19.99**

The Spirituality of Welcoming: How to Transform Your Congregation into a
Sacred Community By Dr. Ron Wolfson 6 x 9, 224 pp, Quality PB, 978-1-58023-244-9 **$19.99**

Rethinking Synagogues: A New Vocabulary for Congregational Life
By Rabbi Lawrence A. Hoffman 6 x 9, 240 pp, Quality PB, 978-1-58023-248-7 **$19.99**

Children's Books

What You Will See Inside a Synagogue
By Rabbi Lawrence A. Hoffman and Dr. Ron Wolfson; Full-color photos by Bill Aron
A colorful, fun-to-read introduction that explains the ways and whys of Jewish
worship and religious life.
8½ x 10½, 32 pp, Full-color photos, HC, 978-1-59473-012-2 **$17.99** For ages 6 & up (A SkyLight Paths book)

The Kids' Fun Book of Jewish Time
By Emily Sper 9 x 7½, 24 pp, Full-color illus., HC, 978-1-58023-311-8 **$16.99**

In God's Hands
By Lawrence Kushner and Gary Schmidt 9 x 12, 32 pp, HC, 978-1-58023-224-1 **$16.99**

Because Nothing Looks Like God
By Lawrence and Karen Kushner
Introduces children to the possibilities of spiritual life.
11 x 8½, 32 pp, Full-color illus., HC, 978-1-58023-092-6 **$16.95** For ages 4 & up

Also Available: **Because Nothing Looks Like God Teacher's Guide**
8½ x 11, 22 pp, PB, 978-1-58023-140-4 **$6.95** For ages 5–8

Board Book Companions to Because Nothing Looks Like God
5 x 5, 24 pp, Full-color illus., SkyLight Paths Board Books For ages 0–4

What Does God Look Like? 978-1-893361-23-2 **$7.99**

How Does God Make Things Happen? 978-1-893361-24-9 **$7.95**

Where Is God? 978-1-893361-17-1 **$7.99**

The Book of Miracles: A Young Person's Guide to Jewish Spiritual Awareness
By Lawrence Kushner. All-new illustrations by the author
6 x 9, 96 pp, 2-color illus., HC, 978-1-879045-78-1 **$16.95** For ages 9 and up

In Our Image: God's First Creatures
By Nancy Sohn Swartz 9 x 12, 32 pp, Full-color illus., HC, 978-1-879045-99-6 **$16.95** For ages 4 & up

Also Available as a Board Book: **How Did the Animals Help God?**
5 x 5, 24 pp, Board, Full-color illus., 978-1-59473-044-3 **$7.99** For ages 0–4 (A SkyLight Paths book)

Holidays/Holy Days

Rosh Hashanah Readings: Inspiration, Information and Contemplation
Yom Kippur Readings: Inspiration, Information and Contemplation
Edited by Rabbi Dov Peretz Elkins with Section Introductions from Arthur Green's These Are the Words
An extraordinary collection of readings, prayers and insights that enable the modern worshiper to enter into the spirit of the High Holy Days in a personal and powerful way, permitting the meaning of the Jewish New Year to enter the heart.
RHR: 6 x 9, 400 pp, HC, 978-1-58023-239-5 **$24.99**
YKR: 6 x 9, 368 pp, HC, 978-1-58023-271-5 **$24.99**

Jewish Holidays: A Brief Introduction for Christians
By Rabbi Kerry M. Olitzky and Rabbi Daniel Judson
5½ x 8½, 144 pp, Quality PB, 978-1-58023-302-6 **$16.99**

Leading the Passover Journey: The Seder's Meaning Revealed, the Haggadah's Story Retold *By Rabbi Nathan Laufer*
Uncovers the hidden meaning of the Seder's rituals and customs.
6 x 9, 224 pp, HC, 978-1-58023-211-1 **$24.99**

Reclaiming Judaism as a Spiritual Practice: Holy Days and Shabbat
By Rabbi Goldie Milgram
7 x 9, 272 pp, Quality PB, 978-1-58023-205-0 **$19.99**

7th Heaven: Celebrating Shabbat with Rebbe Nachman of Breslov
By Moshe Mykoff with the Breslov Research Institute
5⅛ x 8¼, 224 pp, Deluxe PB w/flaps, 978-1-58023-175-6 **$18.95**

The Women's Passover Companion: Women's Reflections on the Festival of Freedom *Edited by Rabbi Sharon Cohen Anisfeld, Tara Mohr, and Catherine Spector*
Groundbreaking. A provocative conversation about women's relationships to Passover as well as the roots and meanings of women's seders.
6 x 9, 352 pp, Quality PB, 978-1-58023-231-9 **$19.99**

The Women's Seder Sourcebook: Rituals & Readings for Use at the Passover Seder *Edited by Rabbi Sharon Cohen Anisfeld, Tara Mohr, and Catherine Spector*
Gathers the voices of more than one hundred women in readings, personal and creative reflections, commentaries, blessings, and ritual suggestions that can be incorporated into your Passover celebration.
6 x 9, 384 pp, Quality PB, 978-1-58023-232-6 **$19.99**

Creating Lively Passover Seders: A Sourcebook of Engaging Tales, Texts & Activities
By David Arnow, PhD 7 x 9, 416 pp, Quality PB, 978-1-58023-184-8 **$24.99**

Hanukkah, 2nd Edition: The Family Guide to Spiritual Celebration
By Dr. Ron Wolfson. Edited by Joel Lurie Grishaver.
7 x 9, 240 pp, illus., Quality PB, 978-1-58023-122-0 **$18.95**

The Jewish Family Fun Book: Holiday Projects, Everyday Activities, and Travel Ideas with Jewish Themes *By Danielle Dardashti and Roni Sarig. Illus. by Avi Katz.*
6 x 9, 288 pp, 70+ b/w illus. & diagrams, Quality PB, 978-1-58023-171-8 **$18.95**

The Jewish Gardening Cookbook: Growing Plants & Cooking for Holidays & Festivals *By Michael Brown* 6 x 9, 224 pp, 30+ b/w illus., Quality PB, 978-1-58023-116-9 **$16.95**

The Jewish Lights Book of Fun Classroom Activities: Simple and Seasonal Projects for Teachers and Students *By Danielle Dardashti and Roni Sarig*
6 x 9, 240 pp, Quality PB, 978-1-58023-206-7 **$19.99**

Passover, 2nd Edition: The Family Guide to Spiritual Celebration
By Dr. Ron Wolfson with Joel Lurie Grishaver 7 x 9, 352 pp, Quality PB, 978-1-58023-174-9 **$19.95**

Shabbat, 2nd Edition: The Family Guide to Preparing for and Celebrating the Sabbath
By Dr. Ron Wolfson 7 x 9, 320 pp, illus., Quality PB, 978-1-58023-164-0 **$19.99**

Sharing Blessings: Children's Stories for Exploring the Spirit of the Jewish Holidays
By Rahel Musleah and Rabbi Michael Klayman
8½ x 11, 64 pp, Full-color illus., HC, 978-1-879045-71-2 **$18.95** *For ages 6 & up*

Spirituality

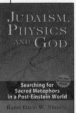

The Adventures of Rabbi Harvey: A Graphic Novel of Jewish Wisdom and Wit in the Wild West *By Steve Sheinkin*
Jewish and American folktales combine in this witty and original graphic novel collection. Creatively retold and set on the western frontier of the 1870s.
6 x 9, 144 pp, Full-color illus., Quality PB, 978-1-58023-310-1 **$16.99**
Also Available: **The Adventures of Rabbi Harvey Teacher's Guide**
8½ x 11, 32 pp, PB, 978-1-58023-326-2 **$8.99**

Ethics of the Sages: *Pirke Avot*—Annotated & Explained
Translation and Annotation by Rabbi Rami Shapiro
5½ x 8½, 192 pp, Quality PB, 978-1-59473-207-2 **$16.99** *(A SkyLight Paths book)*

A Book of Life: Embracing Judaism as a Spiritual Practice
By Michael Strassfeld 6 x 9, 528 pp, Quality PB, 978-1-58023-247-0 **$19.99**

Meaning and Mitzvah: Daily Practices for Reclaiming Judaism through Prayer, God, Torah, Hebrew, Mitzvot and Peoplehood *By Rabbi Goldie Milgram*
7 x 9, 336 pp, Quality PB, 978-1-58023-256-2 **$19.99**

The Soul of the Story: Meetings with Remarkable People
By Rabbi David Zeller 6 x 9, 288 pp, HC, 978-1-58023-272-2 **$21.99**

Aleph-Bet Yoga: Embodying the Hebrew Letters for Physical and Spiritual Well-Being
By Steven A. Rapp. Foreword by Tamar Frankiel, PhD and Judy Greenfeld. Preface by Hart Lazer.
7 x 10, 128 pp, b/w photos, Quality PB, Layflat binding, 978-1-58023-162-6 **$16.95**

Entering the Temple of Dreams: Jewish Prayers, Movements, and Meditations for the End of the Day *By Tamar Frankiel, PhD, and Judy Greenfeld*
7 x 10, 192 pp, illus., Quality PB, 978-1-58023-079-7 **$16.95**

Does the Soul Survive? A Jewish Journey to Belief in Afterlife, Past Lives & Living with Purpose *By Rabbi Elie Kaplan Spitz; Foreword by Brian L. Weiss, MD*
6 x 9, 288 pp, Quality PB, 978-1-58023-165-7 **$16.99**

First Steps to a New Jewish Spirit: Reb Zalman's Guide to Recapturing the Intimacy & Ecstasy in Your Relationship with God *By Rabbi Zalman M. Schachter-Shalomi with Donald Gropman* 6 x 9, 144 pp, Quality PB, 978-1-58023-182-4 **$16.95**

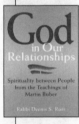

God in Our Relationships: Spirituality between People from the Teachings of Martin Buber *By Rabbi Dennis S. Ross* 5½ x 8½, 160 pp, Quality PB, 978-1-58023-147-3 **$16.95**

Judaism, Physics and God: Searching for Sacred Metaphors in a Post-Einstein World
By Rabbi David W. Nelson 6 x 9, 368 pp, Quality PB, inc. reader's discussion guide, 978-1-58023-306-4 **$18.99**;
HC, 352 pp, 978-1-58023-252-4 **$24.99**

The Jewish Lights Spirituality Handbook: A Guide to Understanding, Exploring & Living a Spiritual Life *Edited by Stuart M. Matlins*
What exactly is "Jewish" about spirituality? How do I make it a part of my life?
Fifty of today's foremost spiritual leaders share their ideas and experience with us.
6 x 9, 456 pp, Quality PB, 978-1-58023-093-3 **$19.99**

Bringing the Psalms to Life: How to Understand and Use the Book of Psalms
By Daniel F. Polish 6 x 9, 208 pp, Quality PB, 978-1-58023-157-2 **$16.95**;
HC, 978-1-58023-077-3 **$21.95**

God & the Big Bang: Discovering Harmony between Science & Spirituality
By Daniel C. Matt 6 x 9, 216 pp, Quality PB, 978-1-879045-89-7 **$16.99**

Minding the Temple of the Soul: Balancing Body, Mind, and Spirit through Traditional Jewish Prayer, Movement, and Meditation *By Tamar Frankiel, PhD, and Judy Greenfeld*
7 x 10, 184 pp, illus., Quality PB, 978-1-879045-64-4 **$16.95**
Audiotape of the Blessings and Meditations: 60 min. **$9.95**
Videotape of the Movements and Meditations: 46 min. **$20.00**

One God Clapping: The Spiritual Path of a Zen Rabbi *By Alan Lew with Sherril Jaffe*
5½ x 8½, 336 pp, Quality PB, 978-1-58023-115-2 **$16.95**

There Is No Messiah ... and You're It: The Stunning Transformation of Judaism's Most Provocative Idea *By Rabbi Robert N. Levine, DD*
6 x 9, 192 pp, Quality PB, 978-1-58023-255-5 **$16.99**

These Are the Words: A Vocabulary of Jewish Spiritual Life
By Arthur Green 6 x 9, 304 pp, Quality PB, 978-1-58023-107-7 **$18.95**

Inspiration

God's To-Do List: 103 Ways to Be an Angel and Do God's Work on Earth
By Dr. Ron Wolfson 6 x 9, 150 pp, Quality PB, 978-1-58023-301-9 **$15.99**

God in All Moments: Mystical & Practical Spiritual Wisdom from Hasidic Masters
Edited and translated by Or N. Rose with Ebn D. Leader
5½ x 8½, 192 pp, Quality PB, 978-1-58023-186-2 **$16.95**

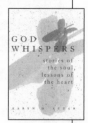

Our Dance with God: Finding Prayer, Perspective and Meaning in the Stories of Our
Lives *By Karyn D. Kedar* 6 x 9, 176 pp, Quality PB, 978-1-58023-202-9 **$16.99**
Also Available: **The Dance of the Dolphin** (HC edition of *Our Dance with God*)
6 x 9, 176 pp, HC, 978-1-58023-154-1 **$19.95**

The Empty Chair: Finding Hope and Joy—Timeless Wisdom from a Hasidic Master,
Rebbe Nachman of Breslov *Adapted by Moshe Mykoff and the Breslov Research Institute*
4 x 6, 128 pp, 2-color text, Deluxe PB w/flaps, 978-1-879045-67-5 **$9.95**

The Gentle Weapon: Prayers for Everyday and Not-So-Everyday Moments—
Timeless Wisdom from the Teachings of the Hasidic Master, Rebbe Nachman of Breslov
Adapted by Moshe Mykoff and S. C. Mizrahi, together with the Breslov Research Institute
4 x 6, 144 pp, 2-color text, Deluxe PB w/flaps, 978-1-58023-022-3 **$9.99**

God Whispers: Stories of the Soul, Lessons of the Heart *By Karyn D. Kedar*
6 x 9, 176 pp, Quality PB, 978-1-58023-088-9 **$15.95**

An Orphan in History: One Man's Triumphant Search for His Jewish Roots
By Paul Cowan; Afterword by Rachel Cowan. 6 x 9, 288 pp, Quality PB, 978-1-58023-135-0 **$16.95**

Restful Reflections: Nighttime Inspiration to Calm the Soul, Based on Jewish Wisdom
By Rabbi Kerry M. Olitzky & Rabbi Lori Forman 4½ x 6½, 448 pp, Quality PB, 978-1-58023-091-9 **$15.95**

Sacred Intentions: Daily Inspiration to Strengthen the Spirit, Based on Jewish Wisdom
By Rabbi Kerry M. Olitzky and Rabbi Lori Forman 4½ x 6½, 448 pp, Quality PB, 978-1-58023-061-2 **$15.95**

Kabbalah/Mysticism/Enneagram

Awakening to Kabbalah: The Guiding Light of Spiritual Fulfillment
By Rav Michael Laitman, PhD 6 x 9, 192 pp, HC, 978-1-58023-264-7 **$21.99**

Seek My Face: A Jewish Mystical Theology *By Arthur Green*
6 x 9, 304 pp, Quality PB, 978-1-58023-130-5 **$19.95**

Zohar: Annotated & Explained
Translation and annotation by Daniel C. Matt; Foreword by Andrew Harvey
5½ x 8½, 176 pp, Quality PB, 978-1-893361-51-5 **$15.99** *(A SkyLight Paths book)*

Cast in God's Image: Discover Your Personality Type Using the Enneagram and Kabbalah
By Rabbi Howard A. Addison
7 x 9, 176 pp, Quality PB, Layflat binding, 20+ journaling exercises, 978-1-58023-124-4 **$16.95**

Ehyeh: A Kabbalah for Tomorrow
By Arthur Green 6 x 9, 224 pp, Quality PB, 978-1-58023-213-5 **$16.99**

The Enneagram and Kabbalah, 2nd Edition: Reading Your Soul
By Rabbi Howard A. Addison 6 x 9, 192 pp, Quality PB, 978-1-58023-229-6 **$16.99**

Finding Joy: A Practical Spiritual Guide to Happiness *By Dannel I. Schwartz with Mark Hass*
6 x 9, 192 pp, Quality PB, 978-1-58023-009-4 **$14.95**

The Flame of the Heart: Prayers of a Chasidic Mystic *By Reb Noson of Breslov. Translated by
David Sears with the Breslov Research Institute* 5 x 7¼, 160 pp, Quality PB, 978-1-58023-246-2 **$15.99**

The Gift of Kabbalah: Discovering the Secrets of Heaven, Renewing Your Life on Earth
By Tamar Frankiel, PhD 6 x 9, 256 pp, Quality PB, 978-1-58023-141-1 **$16.95;**
HC, 978-1-58023-108-4 **$21.95**

Kabbalah: A Brief Introduction for Christians
By Tamar Frankiel, PhD 5½ x 8½, 208 pp, Quality PB, 978-1-58023-303-3 **$16.99**

The Lost Princess and Other Kabbalistic Tales of Rebbe Nachman of Breslov
The Seven Beggars and Other Kabbalistic Tales of Rebbe Nachman of Breslov
Translated by Rabbi Aryeh Kaplan; Preface by Rabbi Chaim Kramer
Lost Princess: 6 x 9, 400 pp, Quality PB, 978-1-58023-217-3 **$18.99**
Seven Beggars: 6 x 9, 192 pp, Quality PB, 978-1-58023-250-0 **$16.99**

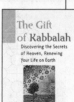

See also *The Way Into Jewish Mystical Tradition* at www.jewishlights.com

About Jewish Lights

People of all faiths and backgrounds yearn for books that attract, engage, educate, and spiritually inspire.

Our principal goal is to stimulate thought and help all people learn about who the Jewish People are, where they come from, and what the future can be made to hold. While people of our diverse Jewish heritage are the primary audience, our books speak to people in the Christian world as well and will broaden their understanding of Judaism and the roots of their own faith.

We bring to you authors who are at the forefront of spiritual thought and experience. While each has something different to say, they all say it in a voice that you can hear.

Our books are designed to welcome you and then to engage, stimulate, and inspire. We judge our success not only by whether or not our books are beautiful and commercially successful, but by whether or not they make a difference in your life.

For your information and convenience, at the back of this book we have provided a list of other Jewish Lights books you might find interesting and useful. They cover all the categories of your life:

Bar/Bat Mitzvah
Bible Study / Midrash
Children's Books
Congregation Resources
Current Events / History
Ecology
Fiction: Mystery, Science Fiction
Grief / Healing
Holidays / Holy Days
Inspiration
Kabbalah / Mysticism / Enneagram

Life Cycle
Meditation
Parenting
Prayer
Ritual / Sacred Practice
Spirituality
Theology / Philosophy
Travel
12-Step
Women's Interest

Stuart M. Matlins

Stuart M. Matlins, Publisher

Or phone, fax, mail or e-mail to: **JEWISH LIGHTS Publishing**
Sunset Farm Offices, Route 4 • P.O. Box 237 • Woodstock, Vermont 05091
Tel: (802) 457-4000 • Fax: (802) 457-4004 • www.jewishlights.com
Credit card orders: (800) 962-4544 (8:30AM–5:30PM ET Monday–Friday)
Generous discounts on quantity orders. SATISFACTION GUARANTEED. Prices subject to change.

For more information about each book, visit our website at www.jewishlights.com